P9-CDY-299

A Compendium of

INDISPENSABLE

FACTS

A Compendium of
INDISPENSABLE
FACTS

by Ben Horslen

BARNES
& NOBLE
BOOKS

NEW YORK

This edition published by Barnes & Noble, Inc.,
by arrangement with Toucan Books Ltd.

2004 Barnes & Noble Books

M 10 9 8 7 6 5 4 3 2 1

ISBN 0-7607-5606-6

Contributing authors: Jacob Field, Ben Horslen,
Cynthia O'Brien, Debbie Robertson, Giles Sparrow
Cover design: Bradbury and Williams
Page design: Joyce Mason
Managing editor: Ellen Dupont
Editor: Marion Dent
Designer: Vivian Foster
Picture researcher: Christine Vincent
Proofreader: Theresa Bebbington

Printed in Dubai

Personally I never care for fiction or storybooks. What I like to read about are facts and statistics of any kind.
… facts, or what a man believes to be facts, are always delightful…
Get your facts first, and then you can distort 'em as much as you please.

Mark Twain (1835–1910)

HUMAN BODY FACTS

Number of hairs shed in a year *30,000*
Brain's average weight *3 lb (1.4 kg)*
Hardest substance *Tooth enamel*
Amount of dead skin shed in a year *9 lb (4 kg)*
Number of times heart beats per year *36.5 million*
Time it takes blood to circulate *23 seconds*
Average stomach capacity *2-2½ pints (0.94-1.18 liters)*
Length fingernails grow in a year *2 in (5 cm)*
Biggest muscle *Gluteus maximus (in the buttock)*
Smallest cell *Sperm*
Largest cell *Ovum*
Water as percentage of body weight *50-60%*
Number of sweat glands *2.5 million*
Biggest bone *Thigh bone (femur)*
Smallest bone *Stapes (in the middle ear)*
Number of bones in each foot *26*

LASSIE FACTS

First dog to play Lassie—Pal, in *Lassie Come Home*, 1943
Pal's owner—Rudd Weatherwax, animal trainer
Amount Rudd Weatherwax paid for Pal—$10.00
Pal's sex—male*
Pal's bad habit—chasing motorcyles
Pal's first stunt—swimming a raging river then lying down, exhausted
What the director said afterwards—"Pal may have gone into the water,
but it was Lassie that came out!"

* *Male dogs shed less than females in summer, so they look better on screen.*

Real name	*Stage name*
Frederick Austerlitz	Fred Astaire
Betty Joan Perske	Lauren Bacall
Melvin Kaminsky	Mel Brooks
Richard Walter Jenkins	Richard Burton
Nicholas Coppola	Nicholas Cage
Maurice Mickelwhite	Michael Caine
Chan Kwong-Sang	Jackie Chan
Vincent Furnier	Alice Cooper
Lucille Le Sueur	Joan Crawford
Bernard Schwartz	Tony Curtis
Doris von Kappelhoff	Doris Day
Issur Danielovitch	Kirk Douglas
Robert Zimmerman	Bob Dylan
Greta Gustafsson	Greta Garbo
Frances Gumm	Judy Garland
Caryn Johnson	Whoopi Goldberg
James Stewart	Stewart Granger
Archie Leach	Cary Grant
Margarita Cansino	Rita Hayworth
William Henry Pratt	Boris Karloff
Arthur Stanley Jefferson	Stan Laurel
Norma Jean Mortenson	Marilyn Monroe
Demetria Guynes	Demi Moore
Joe Yule, Jr	Mickey Rooney
Ramon Estevez	Martin Sheen
Annie Mae Bullock	Tina Turner
Marion Michael Morrison	John Wayne
Jerome Silberman	Gene Wilder

NOUNS OF ASSEMBLAGE

A troop of kangaroos

An ambush of widows
A bask of crocodiles
A college of cardinals
A deceit of lapwings
A dignity of canons
A diligence of messengers
An earth of foxes
A flourish of strumpets
A galaxy of astronomers
A grist of grain
A haggle of shopkeepers
An incredibility of cuckolds
A kennel of hounds
A labor of moles
A multiplying of husbands
An obeisance of servants
A pandemonium of devils
A parade of elephants
A parcel of bachelors
A prudence of vicars
A raft of logs
A rope of onions
A ruck of coal
A scourge of mosquitoes
A sedge of bitterns
A shock of hair
A skulk of thieves
A sownder of swans
A stalk of foresters
A stand of flamingoes
A tabernacle of bakers
A tittering of magpies
An unemployment of graduates
An unkindness of ravens
A walk of snails
A whack of spoils
A yoke of oxen
A zeal of zebras

HARRY POTTER'S FIRST BANQUET AT HOGWARTS SCHOOL

Roast beef, chicken, pork and lamb chops, sausages, bacon, steak, boiled and baked potatoes, French fries, Yorkshire Pudding, peas, carrots, mint humbugs, ice cream, apple pie, treacle tart, chocolate éclairs, jam doughnuts, trifle, strawberries, jello, rice pudding.

Monday

I Don't Like Mondays	Boomtown Rats
Manic Monday	The Bangles
Monday, Monday	The Mamas & Papas
Rainy Days and Mondays	The Carpenters

Tuesday

Love You Till Tuesday	David Bowie
Ruby Tuesday	The Rolling Stones

Wednesday

Wednesday Evening Blues	John Lee Hooker
Wednesday Morning 3 A.M.	Simon and Garfunkel

Thursday

Thursday	Jim Croce
Thursday Afternoon	Brian Eno

Friday

Black Friday	Steely Dan
Friday I'm in Love	The Cure

Saturday

Another Saturday Night	Sam Cooke
Saturday Night	Bay City Rollers

Sunday

I Met Him on a Sunday	Shirelles
Sunday Girl	Blondie

CULTURAL FAUX PAS

The next time you fly off to distant—or not so distant—lands, follow these do's and don'ts. They will help your trip go a little more smoothly (or at least let the natives think you're a cultural sophisticate).

✗ Yawning in Colombia is a no-no.

✗ In India—and other Islamic countries—never serve, pass, or eat food with your left hand. This is considered unhygienic.

✗ Don't take chrysanthemums if invited to dinner in Italy. They're only used at funerals.

✗ Never address a Japanese by his first name. Only family and close friends use this form of address.

✗ Koreans cover their mouths when laughing. You should follow suit.

✗ Showing the soles of your feet in Muslim countries is in bad taste, because the soles are considered the lowest and dirtiest part of the body.

✗ Crossing your fingers in Paraguay is an offensive gesture.

✗ Blinking your eyes at someone in Taiwan will earn you a frown.

✗ Never touch a person's head in Thailand—this is considered the highest and most esteemed part of the body.

✗ Remember that the OK sign in the United States (forefinger and thumb together) is vulgar and obscene in Brazil, impolite in Greece and Russia, means money in Japan, and zero in France.

THE FLAG OF BHUTAN

The flag is divided into two colored sections along a diagonal line from the bottom left to the top right corners. The upper half is saffron-orange, while the lower half is red. In the center of the flag is an oriental dragon.

The oldest, and the smallest, stadium is the Boston Red Sox' Fenway Park, built in 1912. The newest is Citizen's Bank Stadium, where the Philadelphia Phillies will move to for the 2004 season. The biggest stadium is the San Diego Padres' Qualcomm Stadium.

Club	Stadium	Capacity	Date built
Anaheim Angels	Edison International Field	45,090	1966
Arizona Diamondbacks	Bank One Ballpark	49,033	1998
Atlanta Braves	Turner Field	49,831	1997
Baltimore Orioles	Oriole Park at Camden Yards	48,262	1992
Boston Red Sox	Fenway Park	34,218	1912
Chicago Cubs	Wrigley Field	38,902	1914
Chicago White Sox	U.S. Cellular Field	45,936	1991
Cincinnati Reds	Great America Ball Park	42,060	2003
Cleveland Indians	Jacob's Field	43,345	1994
Colorado Rockies	Coors Field	50,381	1993
Detroit Tigers	Comerica Park	40,000	2000
Florida Marlins	Pro Player Stadium	36,331	1987
Houston Astros	Minute Maid Park	40,950	2000
Kansas City Royals	Kauffman Stadium	40,265	1973
Los Angeles Dodgers	Dodger Stadium	56,000	1962
Milwaukee Brewers	Miller Park	43,000	2001
Minnesota Twins	H.H. Humphrey Metrodome	55,883	1982
Montreal Expos	Olympic Stadium	43,739	1975
New York Mets	Shea Stadium	55,601	1964
New York Yankees	Yankee Stadium	57,545	1923
Oakland Athletics	Network Associates Coliseum	48,219	1966
Philadelphia Phillies	Citizen's Bank Park	43,000	2004
Pittsburgh Pirates	PNC Park	38,365	2001
St. Louis Cardinals	Busch Memorial Stadium	60,000	1966
San Diego Padres	Qualcomm Stadium	67,544	1967
San Francisco Giants	Pacific Bell Park	41,059	2000
Seattle Mariners	Safeco Field	46,621	1999
Tampa Bay Devil Rays	Tropicana Field	45,000	1990
Texas Rangers	The Ballpark in Arlington	49,115	1994
Toronto Blue Jays	SkyDome	50,516	1989

THE THREE STOOGES

It may come as some surprise to readers unfamiliar with the history of slapstick comedy that there were, in fact, six Stooges. The bulk of the early Stooge films featured Moe, Shemp, and Larry, with Curly stepping in when Shemp went solo in the 1930s (only to rejoin the group in 1946). However, with the deaths of Curly and Shemp in the 1950s, replacement Stooges Joe Besser and Curly-Joe DeRita were drafted in to fill the gaps.

THE SIX STOOGES

Joe Besser (1907–89)	◎	Curly Howard (1903–52)
Curly-Joe DeRita (1909–93)	◎	Moe Howard (1897–1975)
Larry Fine (1902–75)	◎	Shemp Howard (1895–1955)

SOME HANDY KLINGON PHRASES

Hello: *nuqneH**

Yes: *HIja or HISlaH*

No: *ghobe*

Do you speak Klingon?: *tlhIngan Hol Dajatlh'a*

Your mother has a smooth forehead!: *Hab SoSlI' Quch!***

Today is a good day to die!: *Heqhlu'meh QaQ jajvam!****

If winning is not important, why keep score?: *bortaS blr jablu'Dl'reH QaQqu'nay*

To be or not to be, that is the question.: *taH pagh taHbe, DaH mu'tlheghvam vIqelnIS.*****

*   (Literally, 'What do you want?' – as close as a Klingon gets to a polite greeting)

**   A deadly insult

***   Every day is a good day to die if you're a Klingon

**** Klingons hold that Shakespeare was a Klingon

THE SEVEN DWARFS

Name	Hat	Voice
Bashful	Green	Scotty Malttraw
Doc	Mustard	Roy Atwell
Dopey	Purple	None
Grumpy	Brown	Pinto Colvig
Happy	Orange	Otis Harlan
Sleepy	Green	Pinto Colvig
Sneezy	Tan	Billy Gilbert

NOT THE SEVEN DWARFS

In the early days of planning his first animated feature film, *Snow White and the Seven Dwarfs* (1937), Walt Disney struggled to pick his seven supporting characters from an enormous list of potential names. Here are some of the dwarfs who didn't make it to the screen:

Awful, Biggo-Ego, Biggy, Biggy-Wiggy, Blabby, Busy, Chesty, Crabby, Cranky, Daffy, Dippy, Dirty, Dizzy, Doleful, Dumpy, Flabby, Gabby, Gaspy, Gloomy, Goopy, Graceful, Helpful, Hoppy, Hotsy, Hungry, Jaunty, Jumpy, Lazy, Neurtsy, Nifty, Puffy, Sappy, Scrappy, Shifty, Silly, Snappy, Sneezy-Wheezy, Snoopy, Soulful, Strutty, Tearful, Thrifty, Weepy, Wistful, Woeful

THE EIGHT MOONS OF NEPTUNE

Despina, Galatea, Larissa, Naiad, Nereid, Proteus, Thalassa, Triton

SHOELACE LENGTH

Pairs of holes	Length (in/cm)
2	18/45
3	18/45 or 24/60
4	24/60
5	30/75
6	36/90 or 44/110
8	60/150
9	72/180

TOP TEN DOG BREEDS AROUND THE WORLD

US

Labrador retriever
Golden retriever
German shepherd
Beagle
Dachshund
Yorkshire terrier
Boxer
Poodle
Chihuahua
Shih Tzu

UK

Labrador retriever
German shepherd
Cocker spaniel
English springer spaniel
Staffordshire bull terrier
Golden retriever
West Highland white terrier
Cavalier King
Charles spaniel
Boxer
Rottweiler

GERMANY

German shepherd
Dachshund
Deutsch Drahthaar
Poodle
Boxer
Cocker spaniel
Great Dane
West Highland white terrier
Rottweiler
Golden retriever

FRANCE

German shepherd
Labrador retriever
Yorkshire terrier
English setter
Breton spaniel
Rottweiler
Beauceron
Golden retriever
Cocker spaniel
West Highland white terrier

Many everyday phrases have come down through the generations to become accepted parts of our day-to-day language. But where did they come from in the first place?

A bee in one's bonnet

This curious phrase was first documented in 1845 in the writings of Thomas De Quincey (1785–1859) but, prior to this, 16th-century speakers would have referred to "maggots in the head."

Couch potato

This descriptive term for the TV generation was first coined by American Tom Iacino and then used as a visual joke by fellow American Robert Armstrong in a 1976 cartoon.

Hue and cry

This old phrase was first adapted from the 13th-century French *hu e cri*. The French word *huer* means to make a hooting noise. It was once used when in pursuit of a suspect.

Red herring

Herrings were once used to train hunting dogs. The well-trained dog would continue following the scent of the fox it was chasing, rather than switching to the false trail of the herring. The fish was used because of its strong smell. Nowadays, a red herring refers to any distracting, ultimately unimportant issue or fact.

Steal someone's thunder

An 18th-century playwright, John Dennis (1657–1734), devised a method of imitating the sound of thunder for one of his plays. He later heard the sound used in another production—not his own— and shouted: "Damn them! They will not let my play run, but they steal my thunder."

FIRST NAMES

Names go in and out of fashion, some like Joseph reappearing again and again, others like Emma making a comeback after decades. Boys' names were once utterly predictable— John remained at no. 1 for over 50 years from the 1880s through the 1920s. Parents are often more adventurous with girls' names, inspired by movie stars and characters on TV.

TOP TEN NAMES IN THE UNITED STATES AND CANADA IN 2003

BOYS			GIRLS	
United States	*Canada*		*United States*	*Canada*
Ethan	Michael		Madison	Emily
Aidan	Nicholas		Emma	Sarah
Caleb	Matthew		Grace	Ashley
Jacob	Jacob		Isabella	Kaitlyn
Alexander	Tyler		Hannah	Jessica
Tyler	Chrisopher		Abigail	Brittany
Logan	Zachery		Olivia	Rachel
Ryan	Ryan		Elizabeth	Megan
Dylan	Joshua		Mackenzie	Brianna
Andrew	John		Alexis	Amanda

President	Burial Place
George Washington	Mt. Vernon, VA
John Adams	Quincy, MA
Thomas Jefferson	Charlottesville, VA
James Madison	Montpelier Station, VA
James Monroe	Richmond, VA
John Quincy Adams	Quincy, MA
Andrew Jackson	The Hermitage near Nashville, TN
Martin Van Buren	Kinderhook, NY
William Henry Harrison	North Bend, OH
John Tyler	Richmond, VA
James Knox Polk	Nashville, TN
Zachary Taylor	Louisville, KY
Millard Fillmore	Buffalo, NY
Franklin Pierce	Concord, NH
James Buchanan	Lancaster, PA
Abraham Lincoln	Springfield, IL
Andrew Johnson	Greeneville, TN
Ulysses Simpson Grant	New York, NY
Rutherford Birchard Hayes	Fremont, OH
James Abram Garfield	Cleveland, OH
Chester Alan Arthur	Albany, NY
Grover Cleveland	Princeton, NJ
Benjamin Harrison	Indianapolis, IN
William McKinley	Canton, OH
Theodore Roosevelt	Osyter Bay, NY
William Howard Taft	Arlington National Cemetery
Woodrow Wilson	Washington National Catherdral
Warren Gamaliel Harding	Marion, OH
Calvin Coolidge	Plymouth, VT
Herbert Clark Hoover	West Branch, IA
Franklin Delano Roosevelt	Hyde Park, NY
Harry S. Truman	Independence, MO
Dwight David Eisenhower	Abilene, KS
John Fitzgerald Kennedy	Arlington National Cemetry
Lyndon Baines Johnson	Stonewall, TX
Richard Milhous Nixon	Yorba Linda, CA

TIDDLYWINKS

Since the mid-1950s, the great game of tiddlywinks has been played
by two pairs of winkers on a 3 x 6-ft (2 x 2-m) felt mat. Although the
ostensible object of the game is to propel all of your winks into the
central pot, or container, a great deal of strategy and skill is required
to prevent your winks falling foul of enemy ambush. Before embarking
on a tiddlywink career, therefore, the novice winker would do well to
become familiar with the basic vocabulary of the game.

●	*Altrincham coffin*	The area close to the pot into which one's winks may be nurdled
●	*Bomb*	To launch one of your winks at a pile of rival winks with harmful intent
●	*Boondock*	To send successfully an opponent's wink a great distance from the pot
●	*Doubleton*	A shot in which one of your winks ends up squopping two rival winks
●	*Nurdle*	To maneuver a wink so close to the pot that it cannot be potted
●	*Pot*	To play one of your winks into the pot
●	*Scrunge*	To pot successfully a wink only to watch it rebound out of the pot again
●	*Squidge-off*	The playing of winks into the middle to decide who starts the game
●	*Squidger*	A plastic disc 1–2 in (2.5–5 cm) in diameter that is used to propel one's winks. A winker may use as many squidgers as desired during the game
●	*Squop*	To cover an opponent's wink. A squopped wink may not be played
●	*Squopped up*	The parlous state of having all your winks squopped and therefore being unable to play
●	*Winker*	One who plays tiddlywinks
●	*Winks*	Plastic counters (two large, four small) for playing

NEWTON'S LAWS (1687)

• A body will remain in a state of rest or continue in a state of constant motion unless acted upon by an external force.

• The rate of change of a body's linear momentum is proportional to, and in the direction of, the force applied to it.

• For every action there is an equal and opposite reaction.

ANCIENT INSULTS (LATIN)

Caudex!
Blockhead!

Es barbarus!
You're a barbarian!

Garrula lingua!
Bigmouth!

Pone ubi sol non lucet!
Stick it where the sun don't shine!

Quid gurgustium!
What a dump!

Stulte!
Stupid!

Tu rattus turpis!
You dirty rat!

Vere furis!
You must be crazy!

SPEED CONVERSION

To convert kilometers per hour (km/h) to miles per hour (mph), multiply by 1.609. To convert miles per hour (mph) to kilometers per hour (km/h), multiply by 0.621.

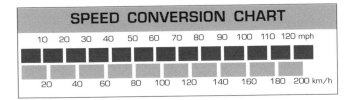

PHOBOPHOBIA AND OTHER PHOBIAS

Ablutophobia: Fear of washing
Achluophobia: Fear of darkness
Bromidrosiphobia: Fear of body smells
Chrometophobia: Fear of money
Enochlophobia: Fear of crowds
Herpetophobia: Fear of reptiles
Iatrophobia: Fear of going to the doctor
Logizomechanophobia: Fear of computers
Ornithophobia: Fear of birds
Peladophobia: Fear of bald people
Phobophobia: Fear of phobias
Selachophobia: Fear of sharks
Tonitrophobia: Fear of thunder

*Ornithophobia is a
fear of birds*

THREE WISE MEN

Name	Kingdom	Gift
Balthazar	Ethiopia	Myrrh
Caspar	Tarsus	Frankincense
Melchior	Arabia	Gold

THE GIFTS GIVEN BY GALADRIEL AT LÓRIEN

In J.R.R. Tolkein's book, *The Lord of the Rings*, all of the fellowship received *lembas* (elf bread), a hood and cloak, a brooch, and ropes made of hithlain, as well as three boats. They used these items to aid them in their search for the ring.

In addition, Galadriel gave each of them a special gift. Frodo received a phial containing the light of "Eärendil's Star," Sam a box filled with earth from Galadriel's orchard, Pippin and Merry small silver belts, Aragorn a sheath for his sword and the Elfstone of the house of Elendil, Boromir a belt of gold, Gimli three strands of Galdriel's hair, and Legolas a new bow and quiver. Gandalf was not present at Lórien, having fallen into the abyss at Moria while fighting a Balrog.

Dr. Johnson's Best Definitions

Samuel Johnson (1709–84) was a masterful British wordsmith—a novelist, critic, essayist, poet, lexicographer, and editor. His definitions ring true even several centuries later.

Apologies are seldom of any use.

Contempt is a kind of gangrene, which if it seizes one part of a character corrupts all the rest by degrees.

Curiosity is one of the permanent and certain characteristics of a vigorous intellect.

Excise A hateful tax levied upon commodities.

Grief is a species of idleness.

Guest A man who stays a week with another and makes him a slave for a week.

Hope is itself a species of happiness and, perhaps, the chief happiness which this world affords.

Lexicographer A writer of dictionaries, a harmless drudge.

Patron Commonly, a wretch who supports with insolence, and is paid with flattery.

Pension Pay given to a state hireling for treason to his country.

Quarks of All Flavors

Most subatomic particles are made of basic units (elementary particles) called quarks, named from the phrase "three quarks for master Mark" in James Joyce's *Finnegan's Wake*. There are six types or "flavors": Up, Down, Strange, Charm, Top, Bottom.

Quarks can combine to form unstable pairs, or stable groups of three. Two up quarks and a down quark make a proton, while two downs and an up make a neutron.

The Flag of Corsica

Adopted by the separatist nationalists of Corsica, the island's flag features a "Maure," or African head, and has a white headband on a white background.

PULITZER PRIZE WINNERS FOR FICTION

The American newspaper publisher Joseph Pulitzer set up The Pulitzer Prizes in 1917 to award achievements in journalism, letters (such as fiction), drama, and music. Here are the fiction winners from 1975 onward.

Year	Author	Title
1975	Michael Shaara	*The Killer of Angels*
1976	Saul Bellow	*Humboldt's Gift*
1977	*no award given*	
1978	James Alan McPherson	*Elbow Room*
1979	John Cheever	*The Stories of John Cheever*
1980	Norman Mailer	*The Executioner's Song*
1981	John Kennedy Toole	*A Confederacy of Dunces*
1982	John Updike	*Rabbit is Rich*
1983	Alice Walker	*The Color Purple*
1984	William Kennedy	*Ironweed*
1985	Alison Lurie	*Foreign Affairs*
1986	Larry McMurtry	*Lonesome Dove*
1987	Peter Taylor	*A Summons to Memphis*
1988	Toni Morrison	*Beloved*
1989	Anne Tyler	*Breathing Lessons*
1990	Oscar Hijuelos	*The Mambo Kings Play Songs of Love*
1991	John Updike	*Rabbit at Rest*
1992	Jane Smiley	*A Thousand Acres*
1993	Robert Olen Butler	*A Good Scent from a Strange Mountain*
1994	E. Annie Proulx	*The Shipping News*
1995	Carol Shields	*The Stone Diaries*
1996	Richard Ford	*Independence Day*
1997	Steven Milhauser	*Martin Dressler: the Tale of an American Dreamer*
1998	Philip Roth	*American Pastoral*
1999	Michael Cunningham	*The Hours*
2000	Jhumpa Lahiri	*Interpreter of Maladies*
2001	Michael Chabon	*The Amazing Adventures of Kavalier & Clay*
2002	Richard Russo	*Empire Falls*
2003	Jeffrey Eugenides	*Middlesex*

THE ESSENTIALS OF ESPERANTO

One of the most unlikely attempts in history to unite mankind under a single banner was begun in 1887 by Polish oculist Dr. L.L. Zamenhof (1859–1917). He created the grammar and vocabulary which he envisioned becoming a global second language—Esperanto.

Esperanto was created with accessibility as its over-riding principle. Zamenhof lived in a small town with four different ethnic groups that shared no common tongue. Drawing on each language spoken in the community, as well as Latin and other major living languages, Zamenhof created an entirely new one, with the aim of eliminating confusion and miscommunication.

In Esperanto, grammar, spelling, and pronunciation are all simple. However, despite its supporters' claims that Esperanto is five times easier to learn than any other language, less than five milliom people speak Esperanto today.

English	Esperanto
Hello	*Saluton*
How are you?	*Kiel vi fartas?*
I love you	*Mi amas vin*
Peace	*Paco*
Thank you	*Dankon*
What time is it?	*Kioma estas la horo?*

CHARLES' LAW

At constant pressure, the volume occupied by a fixed mass of gas is directly proportional to its temperature.

THE MARX BROTHERS

Chico (Leonard, 1886–1961)
Groucho (Julius, 1890–1977)
Gummo (Milton, 1893–1977)
Harpo (Adolph, 1888–1964)
Zeppo (Herbert, 1901–79)

How to Lose Your Marbles

For most common variations of marbles, each player requires five ½-in (13-mm) diameter marbles and one larger shooter or "taw," ¾ in (19 mm) in diameter. The rules of the simplest variant, "Shooting the Ring," are as follows:

The players mark out a chalk circle 6 ft 6 in (2 m) across, and a straight line about 6 ft (1.8m) away from it. Each player places one marble on the perimeter of the circle, arranged so they are roughly equally spaced. Players then roll their shooters toward the center of the ring to determine the order of play—the player closest to the center goes first. Players take turns to shoot, keeping their knees behind the line. The aim is to hit one of the marbles around the circle with enough force to knock both it and the shooter out of the circle. If successful, the player captures the marble and shoots again. If unsuccessful, the player must place another of his/her own marbles on the ring perimeter. Players take turns at shooting until there are no more marbles left on the rim of the circle. The player with the most marbles is then declared the winner.

Truffles

Truffles are the most expensive fungi in the world and many species are found in northern and central Italy. However, only three species of truffle are of any importance in the world of gastronomy. Both the white and black truffles are prized. The third species is mainly used in pastes, patés, or sausages.

1. *Tuber magnatum:* the white truffle or *tartufo d'Alba*
2. *Tuber melanosporum:* the black truffle or *tartufo di Norcia*
3. *Tuber aestivum* or *scozone:* also known as *arufo destate* or *maggengo*

Seven Seas

Antarctic • Arctic • North Atlantic • South Atlantic • Indian Ocean
North Pacific • South Pacific

TYPES OF SNOWFLAKES

Legend has it that no two snowflakes are exactly the same. Even if this is so, snowflakes are not completely unique. All snowflakes fall into one of six basic types:

STAR

The most common type of snowflake is a flat star, usually displaying six-fold symmetry. Star flakes form at temperatures around 5°F (-15°C), settle in light drifts, and fragment easily when they collide with each other or land.

PLATES

A plate is similar in structure to the core of a star flake. It forms in lightly warmer conditions than normal stars, and lack of moisture prevents it forming arms.

DENDRITE

Dendritic snowflakes also have a star shape, but their arms project in a variety of directions, rather than all lying in a flat plane. They form in colder and moister conditions than normal stars.

CAPPED COLUMN

A column with plates at either end of it can form as a flake drops through regions of different temperature and moisture.

COLUMNAR

Column flakes are long, thin, dense, and symmetrical. They form at similar temperatures to stars and dendrites, but in drier conditions.

NEEDLES

Needles form in temperatures only just below freezing, close to the ground. They frequently create a dense snowpack.

INTERNET ACRONYMS

AFK	*Away from keyboard*
BBL	*Be back later*
BBS	*Be back soon*
BCNU	*Be seeing you*
BRB	*Be right back*
BTDT	*Been there, done that*
BTW	*By the way*
FOAF	*Friend of a friend*
FOHCL	*Falls off his/her chair laughing*
FWIW	*For what it's worth*
GMTA	*Great minds think alike*
IMHO	*In my humble opinion*
IOW	*In other words*
IRL	*In real life*
L8R	*[See you] later*
OTOH	*On the other hand*
ROTFL	*Rolls on the floor laughing*
WYSIWYG	*What you see is what you get*

SOUND LEVELS—DECIBELS

0 db	Threshold of audibility
10	Normal breathing
30	Rustling leaves, soft whisper
40	Steady rainfall
60	Face-to-face conversation
70	Vacuum cleaner
80	Ringing telephone
90	Heavy traffic
100	Underground train
110	Live rock concert
120	Pneumatic drill
140	Bicycle horn close-up*
150	Nearby jet engine on takeoff*

* Danger of permanent damage

WIVES OF HENRY VIII

Catherine of Aragon • Anne Boleyn • Jane Seymour
Anne of Cleves • Catherine Howard • Catherine Parr
(divorced, beheaded, died, divorced, beheaded, survived)

DERBY WINNERS

Year	Kentucky	Epsom
1970	Dust Commander	Nijinksy
1971	Canonero II	Mill Reef
1972	Riva Ridge	Roberto
1973	Secretariat	Morston
1974	Cannonade	Snow Knight
1975	Foolish Pleasure	Grundy
1976	Bold Forbes	Empery
1977	Seattle Slew	The Minstrel
1978	Affirmed	Shirley Heights
1979	Spectacular Bid	Troy
1980	Genuine Risk	Henbit
1981	Pleasant Colony	Shergar
1982	Gato Del Sol	Golden Fleece
1983	Sunny's Halo	Teenoso
1984	Swale	Secreto
1985	Spend A Buck	Slip Anchor
1986	Ferdinand	Shahranstani
1987	Alysheba	Reference Point
1988	Winning Colors	Kahyasi
1989	Sunday Silence	Nashwan
1990	Unbridled	Quest for Fame
1991	Strike The Gold	Generous
1992	Lil E. Tee	Dr. Devious
1993	Sea Hero	Commander in Chief
1994	Go For Gin	Erhaab
1995	Thunder Gulch	Lammtarra
1996	Grindstone	Shaamit
1997	Silver Charm	Benny the Dip
1998	Real Quiet	High-Rise
1999	Charismatic	Oath
2000	Fusaichi Pegasus	Sinndar
2001	Monarchos	Galileo
2002	War Emblem	High Chaparral
2003	Funny Cide	Kris Kin

FICTITIOUS FISHING

Despite its title, *The Girl's Guide to
Hunting and Fishing* by Melissa Bank
is not about fishing (or indeed
hunting). However, fans
of fishing can turn to these other
fine works of fiction.

Captains Courageous	Rudyard Kipling
The Compleat Angler, Or the	Izaak Walton*
Contemplative Man's Recreation	
Double Whammy	Carl Hiaasen
Jaws	Peter Benchley
Moby Dick	Herman Melville
The Old Man and the Sea	Ernest Hemingway
A River Runs Through It	Norman Maclean
The Shipping News	E. Annie Proulx
White Eagles Over Serbia	Lawrence Durrell

* *Nonfiction, but no list of fishing books is "compleat" without it.*

OLD-FASHIONED MEASURES

How much of a fruit or vegetable made up a bushel depended on
which one was being measured. Your ancestors would know that you
would need the following amounts to equal a bushel:

60 pounds apples	◎	55 pounds parsnips
52 pounds beans	◎	50 pounds potatoes
24 pounds beets	◎	60 pounds string beans
56 pounds carrots	◎	60 pounds sweet potatoes
54 pounds onions	◎	48 pounds tomatoes

Obscure Proverbs

The bread and butter of mothers-in-law and smug uncles since time immemorial, proverbial wisdom has kept us informed that a rolling stone gathers no moss and you can't have your cake and eat it. However, beyond the everyday truisms with which we are all familiar lie some proverbs whose meanings are not so obvious.

Proverb	Meaning
A bird in the hand is worth two in the bush	Possession is better than expectation
A creaking door hangs longest	Used to comfort the elderly or infirm
A dog who will fetch a bone will carry a bone	One who gossips will take news both ways
All is fish that comes to the net	Everything can be turned to advantage
Better to wed over the mixen than over the moor	Better to marry a neighbor than a stranger
Fine words will butter no parsnips	Words alone will not do
Full cup, steady hand	Don't spoil a good situation through carelessness
The higher the monkey climbs, the more he shows his tail	As an unsuitable person rises, their shortcomings become obvious
When all fruit fails, welcome haws	If you can't marry well, marry someone

ACTORS WHO HAVE PLAYED HERCULE POIROT

The most famous Belgian in fiction, Hercule Poirot first appeared in Agatha Christie's debut novel *The Mysterious Affair at Styles* (1920). The moustachioed sleuth solved cases in 33 novels and five collections of short stories in a career that spanned six decades before his exasperated creator (who had never liked Poirot) finally killed him off in *Curtain* (1975). On screen, Poirot has been portrayed in Christie mysteries by seven actors.

Austin Trevor	*Alibi* (1931), *Black Coffee* (1931), *Lord Edgeware Dies* (1934)
Martin Gabel	*Hercule Poirot* (1962)*
Tony Randall	*The Alphabet Murders* (1966)
Albert Finney	*Murder on the Orient Express* (1974)
Peter Ustinov	*Death on the Nile* (1978), *Evil Under the Sun* (1982), *Thirteen at Dinner* (1985)*, *Dead Man's Folly* (1986)*, *Murder in Three Acts* (1986)*, *Appointment with Death* (1988)
David Suchet	*Agatha Christie's Poirot* (1989–2003)*
Alfred Molina	*Murder on the Orient Express* (2002)*

* Denotes made for television

HOW TO TELL AN AFRICAN FROM AN INDIAN ELEPHANT

African elephants are generally larger than the Indian variety, with larger ears and a concave curve to their back. Indian elephants have a humped back, and only one bump or process on the end of their trunk for grasping objects—African elephants have two.

HOOKE'S LAW

In an elastic material that remains within its limit of elasticity, the stress applied to the material is directly proportional to the strain (stretching) it undergoes.

THE CREATION OF THE WORLD ACCORDING TO THE BIBLE

Day 1 Light
Day 2 Heaven
Day 3 Earth, Sea, and Plants
Day 4 Sun, Moon and the Stars
Day 5 Sea Life and Birds
Day 6 Land Animals and Man
Day 7 God rested

OLIVE OIL GRADINGS

Olive oil is graded on its level of acidity: the lower the level of acidity, the more refined the oil will be. Although heat allows more oil to be extracted from the olives, cold-pressed oils are much superior in taste and quality. All olive oil labels should indicate the percentage of acidity, grade of oi,l and its country of origin.

Grade of oil	*Acidity*
• Extra virgin olive oil	max 1%
• Fine virgin olive oil	max 1.5%
• Virgin olive oil	max 3%
• Pure olive oil	max 3% (a blend of different grades of oil)

THE TEN COMMANDMENTS

1 Thou shalt have no other Gods. 2 Thou shalt not make any graven images. 3 Thou shalt not take the Lord's name in vain. 4 Remember the Sabbath day. 5 Honor thy father and mother. 6 Thou shalt not kill. 7 Thou shalt not commit adultery. 8 Thou shalt not steal. 9 Thou shalt not bear false witness against thy neighbor. 10 Thou shalt not covet thy neighbor's house—nor anything that is his.

Chess Terms

The pieces and their moves:

Pawns ✧ The front row of each player's pieces. May move forward by one square each turn, or by two squares when first moved. Pawns can take other pieces diagonally on neighboring squares.

Rooks ✧ The "castles" at each corner of the board, capable of moving an unlimited distance, but only along a straight line.

Knights ✧ Represented by horses, and placed inward of the rooks on the rear rank. The knight's move is an L-shape—two squares forward and one sideways, or two sideways and one forward. The knight is the only piece allowed to jump over others.

Bishops ✧ Start the game inward of the knights. They can only move along diagonals, so each bishop is restricted to squares of a single color.

Queen ✧ The most powerful piece, allowed to move unlimited distances on straight lines or diagonals, though not allowed to jump over other pieces. Starts the game next to the king.

King ✧ The objective of the game is to capture the king. Can move one square in any direction each turn. Starts the game on the rear center square of the board that matches the color of the player's pieces.

The squares and pieces are often abbreviated to allow a highly condensed description of a match. The rooks, knights, and bishops of each side are termed the "'king's" or "queen's" depending on which piece they start closest to. Pawns in front of them are similarly named "king's knight's pawn," etc. Squares of the board are named from the white player's point of view, with rows counted from 1 (white's rear rank) to 8, and columns lettered a to h.

OTHER TERMS:

Castling ♢ If a player has not moved their king or one of their rooks (and there are no other pieces between them), they can perform this maneuver—the king can move two squares along the board toward the rook, while the rook hops over the king to land on the square next to it on the opposite side.

Check ♢ When a player's move means that their opponent's king can be captured on the next move, it is termed "check." The opponent must then use their next move to save their king.

Checkmate ♢ When a player's move traps their opponent's king so that capture on the next move is inevitable wherever the king moves, "checkmate" is announced, and the game is over.

En passant ♢ If a player moves their pawn forward by two squares on its first move and ends up alongside an opposing pawn, the opponent can take the pawn as if the piece had only moved forward by one square.

Pawn promotion, or Queening ♢ If a player has lost their queen, then a pawn that reaches the opposing player's edge of the board may be exchanged for a new queen.

Stalemate ♢ A situation in which neither player can force checkmate, due to the positioning of the pieces or lack of pieces left on the board. In this case, a draw is declared.

FAMOUS APRIL FOOLS

April 1 is known as April Fool's Day. Those unlucky souls whose birthday falls on that date, doubtless suffer through a lifetime of birthday jokes.

George Baker (1931)	☹	Otto von Bismarck (1815)
Lon Chaney (1883)	☹	Ali McGraw (1938)
Jane Powell (1929)	☹	Sergei Rachmaninoff (1873)
Debbie Reynolds (1932)	☹	Edgar Wallace (1875)

THE CASTE SYSTEM

Traditionally, Hindu society is divided into "varnas" (meaning colors) and then subdivided by occupation into "jatis." This is known in the western world as the caste system and affects choices of marriage, jobs, food, and many other things.

In descending order, the caste system works as follows:

Brahmans: priests and professionals

Kshatriyas: rulers, administrators and soldiers

Vaisyas: farmers and merchants

Sudras: artisans

Dalits (formerly "untouchables"): people who perform "unclean" tasks, such as tanning leather and dealing with dead animals

Although the higher castes can be tainted by association with the lower castes, a member of a low-caste group cannot rise in station by associating with somone of a higher caste. However, the afterlife provides a glimmer of hope since there can be movement to another caste upon rebirth, depending on a person's karma.

The thousands of jatis that have evolved also involve strict rules. Marriage between different groups, for example, is legal, but rarely does it occur in practice.

THE STARSHIPS ENTERPRISE

Since 1966, *Star Trek* has featured a variety of different Starships called *Enterprise*. They are:

Designation	Commissioned	Series/Movie	Captain	Played by
NX-01	2151	Enterprise	Jonathan Archer	Scott Bakula
NCC-1701	2245**	The Original Series	Robert April***	
		III—The Search for Spock	Christopher Pike James T. Kirk Spock	Jeffrey Hunter* William Shatner Leonard Nimoy
NCC-1701A	2286	IV—The Voyage Home to VI—The Undiscovered Country	James T. Kirk	William Shatner
NCC-1701B	2293	Star Trek—Generations	John Harriman	Alan Ruck
NCC-1701C	Operational in 2344	Star Trek—The Next Generation (Ep: Yesterday's Enterprise)	Rachel Garrett	Tricia O'Neil
NCC-1701D	2364	Star Trek—The Next Generation	Jean-Luc Picard	Patrick Stewart
		Star Trek—Generations	William Riker Edward Jellico	Jonathan Frakes Ronnie Cox
NCC-1701E	2372	Star Trek—First Contact to Star Trek—Nemesis	Jean-Luc Picard	Patrick Stewart

* pilot episode only   ** refitted 2271   *** did not appear; only mentioned by other characters

MEASURING EARTHQUAKES

The Richter Scale

Earthquakes are traditionally measured on the Richter Scale, invented by US seismologist Charles F. Richter in 1935. The Richter Scale measures the amplitude of shockwaves generated by an earthquake and is logarithmic, a difference of 1 on the Richter Scale indicates a factor of 10 difference in the amplitude of the earthquake waves, and about 30 times more energy actually released in an earthquake. Contrary to popular belief, the Richter Scale is open-ended—it does not stop at 10. Although the Richter Scale does not define the effects of quakes, in reality thousands of earthquakes of around magnitude 2.0 are happening all the time, and are undetectable except with seismographs. In contrast, one earthquake of magnitude 8 or thereabouts (such as San Francisco in 1906) occurs each year—and stronger quakes are much rarer.

The Mercalli Scale

Measures the intensity of an earthquake by its effects on Earth's surface. Although not as well known as the Richter Scale, it was developed earlier—by seismologists Harry Wood and Frank Neumann in 1931.

I Undetectable by humans.
II Felt when standing still.
III Noticed indoors but thought to be a passing truck or similar.
IV Noticeable vibration, often accompanied by rattling dishes.
V Felt by almost everyone. Some windows broken.
VI Moves heavy furniture, causes minor structural damage.
VII Heavier structural damage in badly constructed buildings.
VIII Considerable damage to ordinary buildings. Chimneys collapse, furniture overturned.
IX Buildings shifted off foundations, even if earthquake proof.
X Masonry buildings destroyed, wooden ones damaged.
XI Most buildings and bridges destroyed.
XII Total destruction, general upheaval of landscape.

ORIGINS OF THE DAYS OF THE WEEK

Most of the modern English names for the days of the week can be traced back to Latin, either directly or through the Germanic influence on Old English.

Monday—literally meaning "the moon's day"—comes from a Germanic translation of the Latin "lunae dies" that also gives the modern German "Montag" for the first day of the working week.

Tuesday derives its name from Tiu, a Germanic god of war and the sky ("Tiu's day"). In French, the Roman war god, Mars, lends his name to "Mardi" in the same way.

Wednesday is also named for a Germanic god—Woden (also known as Odin in Norse mythology).

Thursday is a corruption of "Thor's day" (named after the Norse god of thunder).

Friday is named for the Norse goddess of love and fertility Freya ("Freya's day"). The French "Vendredi" follows the same route via the Roman goddess Venus.

Saturday is a direct borrowing from the Latin "Saturni dies" ("Saturn's day"), named for the ancient Roman god of agriculture.

Sunday also takes its name directly from Latin, in this case, "dies solis"—"day of the sun."

RULES OF BOULES

In this outdoor game, two teams, each with two or three players, compete to throw metal balls called *boules* toward a small wooden target ball called a *cochonnet*. The winning team is the one that comes closest to the cochonnet. The game can be played on almost any flat, packed dirt surface, or even grass or tarmac.

Each of 12 boules is marked to help the players identify their own. The first team marks a small circle on the ground in which to stand and toss the cochonnet. The player then throws one of his or her boules, attempting to hit the cochonnet.

The second team then takes turns to throw their boules, aiming to get closer to the cochonnet than the first team's boules—either by landing closer to the target or by knocking an opposing boule out of the way. The players of the first team then take another turn, and the teams continue to alternate until one or both has used up all their boules. If any player hits the cochonnet when the other team has no more boules to play, then that player's team scores a point for each unplayed boule they have left.

The round is won by the team with the boule closest to the cochonnet. They score a point for each boule closer to the cochonnet than any of the opposing team's boules. A player from the winning team then begins the next round by throwing the cochonnet again. The game usually continues until one team's score has reached a total of 13 points.

THE MEANING OF ACRONYMS

Poet's day	Push Off Early, Tomorrow's Saturday
Posh	Port Out, Starboard Home (referring to the shady side of ships favored by the wealthy English families as they traveled to and from India)
Radar	RAdio Detecting And Ranging
RAM	Random-Access Memory
Snafu	Situation Normal (All Fouled Up)

Battery Sizes and Types

Type	*Diameter*	*Height*	*Width*	*Voltage*
AAA	2/5 in/1.05 cm	1 4/5 in/4.45 cm	n/a	1.5V
AA	3/5 in/1.45 cm	2 in/5 cm	n/a	1.5V
C	1 in/2.62 cm	2 in/5 cm	n/a	1.5V
D	1 3/10 in/3.42 cm	2 2/5 in/6.12 cm	n/a	1.5V
9V	n/a	1 9/10 in/4.85 cm	1 2/5 in/3.56 cm	9V

Twitcher Talk

Birder	A birdwatcher
Clinch	To identify a rare specimen
Dip in	To go on a successful twitch (q.v.)
Dude	A casual birdwatcher
Flyway	A major route for migrating birds
Gripped off	Annoyed
Lifer	A species seen for the first time by a birder who can then add it to their "life list"
Lister	A birder who lists every bird he sees
Med	Bird of Mediterranean origin
Sibe	Bird of Siberian origin
Ten Rare Men	The members of the Rarities Committee of the *British Birds* journal
Tick hunter	A particularly committed birder
Twitch	A trip undertaken, often over great distances and with consequent excitement (hence the twitch), to see a particular species of bird
Twitcher	One who undertakes a twitch (often mistakenly used as a synonym for birder)
Unblock	To get even (such as with a fellow birder on your twitch who has previously rendered you gripped off by clinching a hitherto unheard-of Sibe)

BIRTHSTONES

Birthstones are gemstones associated with the different months of the year. They are thought to derive from ancient astrology, and the earliest mention of them comes from the Bible (Exodus Ch.39), where they are described adorning the breastplate of the Hebrew high priest, and associated with the twelve tribes of Israel. Today, the generally accepted list is as follows:

January: Garnet
February: Amethyst
March: Aquamarine or Bloodstone
April: Diamond or Rock Crystal
May: Emerald or Chrysoprase
June: Pearl or Moonstone

July: Ruby or Carnelian
August: Peridot or Sardonyx
September: Sapphire or Lapis Lazuli
October: Opal or Tourmaline
November: Topaz or Citrine
December: Turquoise

SEA SERPENTS

In his book *In the Wake of Sea-Serpents* (1968), Belgian zoologist Bernard Heuvelmans, the founder of the science of cryptozoology (the study of animals still awaiting formal discovery), outlines seven distinct types of sea serpent that are most commonly reported, suggesting seven large new sea creatures awaiting discovery:

Long-necked A beast sighted as simply a long, thin neck with a small head on the end.
Many-finned A creature with large numbers of fins emerging from a long, serpentine body.
Many-humped A creature seen as a row of humps or loops emerging from the water.
Marine-saurian Giant marine reptile, possibly a surviving descendant of plesiosaurs from the era of the dinosaurs.
Merhorse A thicker neck with a larger, horselike head.
Super-eel A giant eel, as its name suggests.
Super-otter A giant otter or seal with a long neck.

BONES OF THE HUMAN BODY

Babies are born with between 275 and 300 separate bones, but many of these fuse together in the first few years of development. An adult human normally has 206 bones. From top to toe, these are:

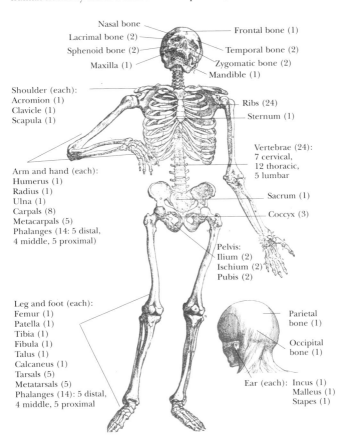

Nasal bone
Lacrimal bone (2)
Sphenoid bone (2)
Maxilla (1)
Frontal bone (1)
Temporal bone (2)
Zygomatic bone (2)
Mandible (1)

Shoulder (each):
Acromion (1)
Clavicle (1)
Scapula (1)

Ribs (24)
Sternum (1)

Vertebrae (24):
7 cervical,
12 thoracic,
5 lumbar

Arm and hand (each):
Humerus (1)
Radius (1)
Ulna (1)
Carpals (8)
Metacarpals (5)
Phalanges (14: 5 distal,
4 middle, 5 proximal)

Sacrum (1)

Coccyx (3)

Pelvis:
Ilium (2)
Ischium (2)
Pubis (2)

Leg and foot (each):
Femur (1)
Patella (1)
Tibia (1)
Fibula (1)
Talus (1)
Calcaneus (1)
Tarsals (5)
Metatarsals (5)
Phalanges (14): 5 distal,
4 middle, 5 proximal

Parietal
bone (1)

Occipital
bone (1)

Ear (each): Incus (1)
Malleus (1)
Stapes (1)

THE TRUE FATE OF THE VON TRAPPS

With the enormous success of the cinematic version of *The Sound of Music* in 1965, it seemed that the precocious child-actors who portrayed the singing Von Trapp children each had a glittering future ahead of them on the silver screen. But where are they now?

Von Trapp	Played by	Where they are now
Liesl	Charmian Carr	Owns her own interior design company in California.
Friedrich	Nicholas Hammond	Still earns a crust as a stage actor in Australia.
Brigitta	Angela Cartwright	Went on to appear in *Lost in Space* but now runs a gift shop.
Louisa	Heather Menzies	Became a full-time mother after starring in *Logan's Run*.
Kurt	Duane Chase	Tests computer software for oil and mining companies.
Marta	Debbie Turner	Is now a housewife in Minnesota.
Gretl	Kym Karath	Made regular appearances on the US TV show *All My Children* before taking time off to have a baby.

THE HARPIES

According to Greek mythology, these winged beings were responsible for carrying people and things away to the "other world." Originally conceived as birds with women's heads, they are shown as winged women from the sixth century onward. The Harpies were Aello, Ocypete, and Celaeno and were believed to be daughters of Thaumas and Electra, the daughter of Ocean.

THE MARSEILLAISE

Originally entitled *Chant de guerre de l'armee du Rhin*, the *Marseillaise* (as it became known due to its popularity with volunteer units from Marseille) was written by Claude-Joseph Rouget de Lisle in 1792. Three years later, the *Marseillaise* was adopted as the French national anthem. Although there are many verses in the full version, the following two are the most commonly sung.

Allons enfants de la Patrie
Le jour de gloire est arrivé.
Contre nous de la tyrannie
L'étendard sanglant est levé,
L'étendard sanglant est levé.
Entendez vous dans les campagnes
Mugir ces féroces soldats.
Ils viennent jusque dans vos bras
Égorger vos fils, vos compagnes.

Arise, children of the fatherland,
The day of glory has come.
Against us the bloodstained
Banner of tyranny is raised,
The banner of tyranny is raised.
Hear, in the fields
The roar of her fierce soldiers.
They come right into our arms
To slaughter your sons and your consorts.

Aux armes citoyens!
Formez vos bataillons!
Marchons, marchons!
Qu'un sang impur abreuve
nos sillons!

Patriots, to arms!
Form your battalions!
Let's march! Let's march!
May the tyrant's foul blood water
our furrows!

THE STATUE OF LIBERTY

The Statue of Liberty was a joint effort between France and the USA, with France building the statue and the USA the pedestal. The statue, made of 31 tons of copper and 125 tons of steel, was transported in 350 pieces aboard the French frigate *Isere*. It was erected in 1886.

THE FLAG OF FRANCE

Known as the tricolor, it has equal-sized vertical stripes of blue (in the hoist), white, and red.

TONGUE TWISTERS

Stupid superstition.

Pirates' Private Property.

Two tried and true tridents.

Tie twine to three tree twigs.

Peggy Babcock.

Bake big batches of bitter brown bread.

This is a zither.

I want a proper cup of coffee in a proper copper coffee pot.

Sally is a sheet slitter, she slits sheets.

A noisy noise annoys an oyster.

Which wristwatches are Swiss wristwatches?

The great Greek grape growers grow great Greek grapes.

I'm not a pheasant plucker,
I'm a pheasant plucker's son,
And I'm only plucking pheasants
'Till the pheasant plucker comes.

Betty Botter had some butter,
 "But," she said, "this
 butter's bitter.
If I bake this bitter butter,
 it would make my batter bitter.
But a bit of better butter, that
 would make my batter better."

To sit in solemn silence in a dull
 dark dock
In a pestilential prison with a life
 long lock
Awaiting the sensation of a short
 sharp shock
From a cheap and chippy
 chopper on a big black block.

How many cans can a cannibal
 nibble?
If a cannibal can nibble cans?

I saw Susie sitting in a shoe shine shop.
Where she sits she shines, and where she shines she sits.

EPONYMOUS WORDS

Eponymous word	Namesake
Celsius (denoting a scale of temperature)	Anders Celsius (1701–44, Swedish astronomer)
Chihuahua (breed of small dog)	Chihuahua state in northeast Mexico
Chippendale (style of furniture)	Thomas Chippendale (1718–79)
Derby (annual horse race at Epsom)	12th Earl of Derby (1752–1834)
Draconian (unnecessarily harsh or brutal)	Draco (Athenian lawyer's code of laws, *c.*621 BC)
Fuchsia (variety of colorful, drooping flower)	Leonhard Fuchs (1501–66, German botanist)
Geiger counter (instrument to measure radioactivity)	Hans Geiger (1882–1945, German physicist)
Guillotine (device of execution)	Joseph Ignace Guillotin (1738–1814, French physician)
Listerine (antiseptic mouthwash)	Joseph Lister (1827–1912)
Lynch (an execution without trial or proper sentencing)	Captain William Lynch (1741–1820)
Masochism (enjoyment of pain)	Leopold von Sacher Masoch (1836–95)
Quixotic (obsessively idealistic)	Don Quixote (fictional character)
Saxophone (musical instrument)	Adolphe Sax (1814–94)
Stradivarius (rare and valuable string instrument, especially violin)	Antonio Stradivari (1644–1737)
Tarmac/Macadam (revolutionary road surfacing material)	John McAdam (1756–1836, Scottish engineer)
Wellington boot (knee-length boot, popularized by the Iron Duke)	Arthur Wellesley, 1st Duke of Wellington (1769–1852)
Winchester (breech-loading rifle)	Oliver Winchester (1810–80)
Zeppelin (airship)	Ferdinand von Zeppelin (1838–1917)

TENNIS SCORING

GAME: The winner of a game is the first person to score four points, but they must lead by two points. The score is announced with the points of whoever is serving read first: Love means zero, the first point is fifteen, the second thirty, the third forty. The fourth point can win the game, but if both players tie on forty–all (deuce), a tiebreak is played in which one player must first win a point to gain advantage, then win the next point for the game. These bizarre names are thought to come from medieval France, where the game originated—the numbers may be associated with the quarter-hours on a clock face.

SET: Players serve in alternate games. The winner of a set is the first person to win six games, but again the winner must take the set by two clear games, so may have to play to 7–5. If the players tie on 6–all, a tiebreak is played, with players serving alternately and using the same scoring system as a set until one player has at least 6 points and leads by 2.

MATCH: Matches are won on either the "best of three" sets (most commonly) or "best of five" (for major men's championships).

US SONGS OF THE CENTURY

The National Endowment for the Arts and the Recording Industry of America have listed these songs as the top 10 of the 20th century:

Over the Rainbow	◎	Judy Garland
White Christmas	◎	Bing Crosby
This land is Your Land	◎	Woodie Guthrie
Respect	◎	Aretha Franklin
American Pie	◎	Don McLean
Boogie Woogie Bugle Boy	◎	The Andrews Sisters
West Side Story (album)	◎	the original cast
Take Me Out to the Ball Game	◎	Billy Murray
You've Lost That Lovin' Feelin	◎	The Righteous Brothers
The Entertainer	◎	Scott Joplin

CHINESE DYNASTIES

Qin 221–206 BC
Western Han 206 BC–AD 23
Eastern Han 25–220

The Three Kingdoms
Wei 220–264
Wu 222–280
Shu Han 221–263

Western Jin 265–316
Eastern Jin 317–419
Liu Song 420–479
Qi 479–501
Liang 502–556
Chen 557–589
Sui 581–618
Tang 618–907

Five Dynasties
Later Liang 907–923
Later Tang 923–935
Later Jin 936–947
Later Han 947–951
Later Zhou 951–960

Northern Song 960–1126
Southern Song 1127–1279
Yuan 1279–1368
Ming 1368–1644
Qing 1644–1911

CONVERSIONS

To convert inches to centimeters, multiply by 2.54.
To convert centimeters to inches, multiply by 0.394.

THE FELLOWSHIP OF THE RING

Wizard
Gandalf

Men
Aragorn (Strider), Boromir

Elf
Legolas

Dwarf
Gimli

Hobbits
Brandybuck, Frodo Baggins,
Gamgee, Meriadoc (Merry),
Peregrin (Pippin) Took,
Samwise (Sam)

STAFF AT HOGWARTS

Prof Binns	History of Magic
Prof Albus Dumbledore	Head
Argus Filch	Caretaker
Firenze	Divination, Book 5
Prof Flitwick	Charms
Prof Grubbly-Plank	Care of Magical Creatures, Books 4 & 5 [temp]
Rubeus Hagrid	Groundskeeper & Care of Magical Creatures, Books 3, 4, & 5
Madam Hooch	Flying
Prof Kettleburn	Care of Magical Creatures, Books 1 & 2
Prof Gilderoy Lockhart	Defence against the Dark Arts, Book 2
Prof Remus J Lupin	Defence against the Dark Arts, Book 3
Prof Minerva McGonagall	Deputy Head & Transfiguration
Prof Alastor 'Mad Eye' Moody	Defence against the Dark Arts, Book 4
Madam Pince	Librarian
Madam Poppy Pomfrey	Nurse
Prof Quirrell	Defence against the Dark Arts, Book 1
Prof Sinistra	Astronomy
Prof Severus Snape	Potions
Prof Sprout	Herbology
Prof Sybill Trelawney	Diviniation
Prof Vector	Arithmancy
Dolores Umbridge	Defence against the Dark Arts, Head Book 5

Breeding Big Cats

Several species of big cats can be interbred in zoos—the most common are tigers and lions, which produce ligers (where the father is a lion), and tigons (where the father is a tiger). Although the female cubs of these crossbreeding experiments are sometimes fertile, the males are invariably sterile.

The following table lists the known combinations:

MALE → FEMALE ↓	Lion	Tiger	Leopard	Jaguar	Puma	Serval	Caracal
Lion	Lion	Tigon	Leopon	X	X	X	X
Tiger	Liger	Tiger	Dogla*	X	X	X	X
Leopard	Marozi*	Tigard**	Leopard	Jagulep	Pumapard	X	X
Jaguar	X	X	X	Jaguar	X	X	X
Puma	X	X	X	Pumaguar*	Puma	X	X
Serval	X	X	X	X	X	Serval	Caraval
Caracal	X	X	X	X	X	Servical	Caracal

*   *Hybrid rumoured to occur naturally in the wild, but not confirmed by science.*

** *Crossbreeding experiment resulted in stillborn cubs.*

COMPASS POINTS

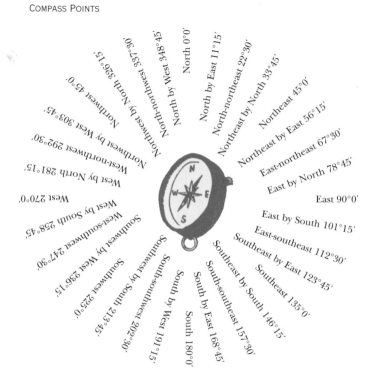

North 0°0'
North by East 11°15'
North-northeast 22°30'
Northeast by North 33°45'
Northeast 45°0'
Northeast by East 56°15'
East-northeast 67°30'
East by North 78°45'
East 90°0'
East by South 101°15'
East-southeast 112°30'
Southeast by East 123°45'
Southeast 135°0'
Southeast by South 146°15'
South-southeast 157°30'
South by East 168°45'
South 180°0'
South by West 191°15'
South-southwest 202°30'
Southwest by South 213°45'
Southwest 225°0'
Southwest by West 236°15'
West-southwest 247°30'
West by South 258°45'
West 270°0'
West by North 281°15'
West-northwest 292°30'
Northwest by West 303°45'
Northwest 315°0'
Northwest by North 326°15'
North-northwest 337°30'
North by West 348°45'

MILLIONS AND BILLIONS (AMERICAN SYSTEM)

Million	1,000,000 = thousand x thousand
Billion	1,000,000,000 = thousand x million
Trillion	1,000,000,000,000 = thousand x billion
Quadrillion	1,000,000,000,000,000 = thousand x trillion

THE CODE OF CHIVALRY

Medieval knights were expected to adhere to a strict code of behavior that was underlined by religious and patriotic values. The courting and protection of comely damsels was a later development of the chivalric tradition. Leon Gautier (1832–87), a French historian, outlined the code in his book *Chivalry, the Everyday Life of a Medieval Knight*.

1. Thou shalt believe all the Church teaches and shalt obey her commandments.
2. Thou shalt defend the Church.
3. Thou shalt respect all weaknesses and shalt constitute thyself the defender of them.
4. Thou shalt love the country in which thou wast born.
5. Thou shalt not recoil before thine enemy.
6. Thou shalt make war against the infidel without cessation and without mercy.
7. Thou shalt perform scrupulously thy feudal duties, if they be not contrary to the laws of God.
8. Thou shalt never lie, and shalt remain faithful to thy pledged word.
9. Thou shalt be generous, and give largesse to everyone.
10. Thou shalt be everywhere and always the champion of the Right and the Good against injustice and Evil.

SUPREME BEINGS

Most religions have a supreme deity, but the name by which this being is known is varied.

Religion	Deity
Christianity	God
Daoism	Man, Mo
Hinduism	Brahma, Durga, Ganesha, Hanuman, Lakshmi, Saraswati, Shriva, Vishnu
Islam	Allah
Judaism	God
Shintoism	Kami (comprised of numerous deities, one of the most popular being Inari)
Sikhism	True Guru
Zoroastrianism	Ahura Mazda

WHODUNNIT IN AGATHA CHRISTIE

Book	Murderer
And Then There Were None	Laurence John Wargrave
Appointment with Death	Lady Westholme
The Body in the Library	Mark Gaskell & Josephine Turner
Cards on the Table	Dr. Roberts & Miss Meredith
Cat Among the Pigeons	Ann Shapland
Crooked House	Josephine Leonides
Death on the Nile	Jacqueline de Bellefort & Simon Doyle
Evil Under the Sun	Patrick Redfern
Five Little Pigs	Elsa Greer
4:50 from Paddington	Dr. Quimper
Murder in Mesopotamia	Dr. Eric Leidner
Nemesis	Clotilde Bradbury-Scott
One, Two, Buckle My Shoe	Alistair Blunt
Peril at End House	Nick Buckley

Tap Dancing Terms

Here are just a few of the simpler steps in tap dancing for the beginner:

Cross turn *Cross and turn; tap, tap, tap*
Cross the right foot in front of the left and keep it very close to the ankle. Rise high on the right foot (half toe) and push the body into a turn toward the left.

Then put the left foot in front of the right and repeat the above motion to complete the turn. Then move the right foot out and tap the floor three times.

Digs *Cross, tap; cross, tap*
Arms out in front. Simply cross your right foot over the left, toe down. Tap the toe on the floor. Repeat with the left foot.

Heel drops *Heel, step; heel, step*
Place your arms in front of your body at chest height. Bend the elbows and place the right arm over the left. The right fingers should be near the left elbow.

Move the right heel a short distance to the front with the toe up off the floor. Bring it back, shifting the weight to the left foot. Shift weight to the right foot and take the left foot out.

Scoot backs *Bend, jump; rise, straighten*
Bend the knees slightly, keep together, and make a jump backward. As you rise up, straighten the knees and stretch out the arms. Sink the knees again and repeat the first step. Then clap as you straighten and rise.

Toe slaps *Slap, step; slap, step*
Hands on hips, rise to the balls of the feet and slap, step with the right foot and then with the left.

Triples *Hop, Brush-Brush* (also known as *The Threes*)
Put the hands on the hips. Shift weight to the left foot. Hop on the left foot and raise the right foot. Do a brush, brush step with the right foot. Then hop on the right foot and do a brush, brush with the left.

GREETINGS AROUND THE WORLD

Generally speaking, a handshake is the universal form of greeting. But there are exceptions or some extra touching involved in some cases.

Belgium Three kisses is the Belgian way, alternating cheeks; this is also true in Switzerland

China A slight bow is appropriate

Greece A handshake followed by an embrace and/or kiss on the first and subsequent meetings

Japan A long, low bow is the norm

Oman Say *salaam alaykum*, shake hands while saying *kaif halak,* and then your host will place his left hand on your right shoulder and kiss you on both cheeks

Tahiti Shaking hands is usual—even if you are in a group of up to 30, you are expected to shake hands with everyone. In addition, Tahitians usually kiss cheeks when greeting one another.

US TOP POP RECORDING ARTISTS

The following records have been achieved by these recording artists:

Most no.1 singles: The Beatles, with 20.

Most no.1 albums by a male solo artist: Elvisy Presley, with nine.

Most successful male solo artist: Garth Brooks, having sold 89 million albums in the United States.

Most successful female solo artist: Madonna, who has sold 120 million albums by November 2000, and with 35 top 10 singles and 12 top 10 albums.

Youngest artist with a no.1 album: Stevie Wonder, at the age of 13, with *Little Stevie Wonder—The Twelve Year Old Genius*

Most successful song-writing duo: John Lennon and Paul McCartney, who co-wrote 23 US no.1 single hits.

Top-selling album: The Eagles' *The Greatest Hits 1971–1975*, which has reached 26 million sales.

Top-selling single: Elton John's *Candle in the Wind 1997,* at 11 million.

THE RULES OF SWORD FIGHTING

The invention of gunpowder in the 14th century brought about the art of sword fighting or fencing. Until then, swords had been used in earnest, on the field of battle. Once swords were used for sport, rather than a way of settling disputes, a rule book was needed. Here are some key regulations:

○ Before the start of a "fight," or bout, the fencers must perform a salute to one another, to the audience, and to the referee. If one of the fencers does not comply, he or she receives a red card
○ Corps à corps—physical contact between the players—is strictly forbidden
○ Irregular movements, such as strikes achieved with violence or while falling, are against all rules
○ Competitors must never turn their backs on one another during a bout
○ Competitors must keep their masks on until the referee calls an end to the bout
○ At the end of an encounter, the fencers again salute one another, the spectators, and the referee.

MORSE CODE

A	• –	M	– –	Y	– • – –
B	– • • •	N	– •	Z	– – • •
C	– • – •	O	– – –	0	– – – – –
D	– • •	P	• – – •	1	• – – – –
E	•	Q	– – • –	2	• • – – –
F	• • – •	R	• – •	3	• • • – –
G	– – •	S	• • •	4	• • • • –
H	• • • •	T	–	5	• • • • •
I	• •	U	• • –	6	– • • • •
J	• – – –	V	• • • –	7	– – • • •
K	– • –	W	• – –	8	– – – • •
L	• – • •	X	– • • –	9	– – – – •

THE CONSTELLATIONS (Alphabetically)

Latin name	Meaning	Abbreviation	Size (square degrees)
Andromeda	Andromeda	And	722
Antlia	The Air Pump	Ant	239
Apus	The Bird of Paradise	Aps	206
Aquarius	The Water Carrier	Aqr	980
Aquila	The Eagle	Aql	652
Ara	The Altar	Ara	237
Aries	The Ram	Ari	441
Auriga	The Charioteer	Aur	657
Boötes	The Herdsman	Boo	907
Caelum	The Chisel	Cae	125
Camelopardalis	The Giraffe	Cam	757
Cancer	The Crab	Cnc	506
Canes Venatici	The Hunting Dogs	CVn	465
Canis Major	The Great Dog	CMa	380
Canis Minor	The Little Dog	CMi	183
Capricornus	The Sea Goat	Cap	414
Carina	The Keel (of Argo)	Car	494
Cassiopeia	Cassiopeia	Cas	598
Centaurus	The Centaur	Cen	1060
Cepheus	Cepheus	Cep	588
Cetus	The Whale	Cet	1231
Chameleon	The Chameleon	Cha	132
Circinus	The Compasses	Cir	93
Columba	The Dove	Col	270
Coma Berenices	Berenice's Hair	Com	386
Corona Australis	The Southern Crown	CrA	128
Corona Borealis	The Northern Crown	CrB	179
Corvus	The Crow	Crv	184
Crater	The Cup	Crt	282
Crux	The (Southern) Cross	Cru	68
Cygnus	The Swan	Cyg	804
Delphinus	The Dolphin	Del	189
Dorado	The Swordfish	Dor	179
Draco	The Dragon	Dra	1083
Equuleus	The Foal	Equ	72
Eridanus	The River	Eri	1138
Fornax	The Furnace	For	398
Gemini	The Twins	Gem	514
Grus	The Crane	Gru	366
Hercules	Hercules	Her	1225
Horologium	The Clock	Hor	249
Hydra	The Water Snake	Hya	1303
Hydrus	The Little Water Snake	Hyi	243

Indus	The Indian	Ind	294
Lacerta	The Lizard	Lac	201
Leo	The Lion	Leo	947
Leo Minor	The Little Lion	LMi	232
Lepus	The Hare	Lep	290
Libra	The Scales	Lib	538
Lupus	The Wolf	Lup	334
Lynx	The Lynx	Lyn	545
Lyra	The Lyre	Lyr	286
Mensa	Table Mountain	Men	153
Microscopium	The Microscope	Mic	210
Monoceros	The Unicorn	Mon	482
Musca	The Fly	Mus	138
Norma	The Level	Nor	165
Octans	The Octant	Oct	291
Ophiuchus	The Serpent Bearer	Oph	948
Orion	Orion, the Hunter	Ori	594
Pavo	The Peacock	Pav	378
Pegasus	Pegasus, the Winged Horse	Peg	1121
Perseus	Perseus	Per	615
Phoenix	The Phoenix	Phe	469
Pictor	The Painter's Easel	Pic	247
Pisces	The Fishes	Psc	889
Piscis Austrinus	The Southern Fish	PsA	245
Puppis	The Stern (of Argo)	Pup	673
Pyxis	The Mariner's Compass	Pyx	221
Reticulum	The Net	Ret	114
Sagitta	The Arrow	Sge	80
Sagittarius	The Archer	Sgr	867
Scorpius	The Scorpion	Sco	497
Sculptor	The Sculptor	Scl	475
Scutum	The Shield	Sct	109
Serpens	The Serpent	Ser	637
Sextans	The Sextant	Sex	314
Taurus	The Bull	Tau	797
Telescopium	The Telescope	Tel	252
Triangulum	The Triangle	Tri	132
Triangulum Australe	The Southern Triangle	TrA	110
Tucana	The Toucan	Tuc	295
Ursa Major*	The Great Bear	UMa	1280
Ursa Minor	The Little Bear	UMi	256
Vela	The Sail (of Argo)	Vel	500
Virgo	The Virgin	Vir	1294
Volans	The Flying Fish	Vol	141
Vulpecula	The Fox	Vul	268

includes The Plough

FOODS NAMED FOR
NATURAL PHENOMENA
Cloudberries
Mud pie
Rainbow trout
Rock cakes
Rock salmon
Snow eggs
Snow peas
Snowball
Starfruit
Sunfish
Tequila Sunrise

FOODS NAMED FOR
PLACES
Baked Alaska
Boston cream pie
Brazil nut
Cheddar cheese
Hamburger
Manhattan clam chowder
Mississippi mud pie
Peking duck
Philadelphia cream cheese
Waldorf salad
Yorkshire pudding

KEPLER'S LAWS OF PLANETARY MOTION
• Every planet orbits the Sun in an ellipse with the Sun at one focus of the ellipse.
• A line drawn between the Sun and a planet will sweep out equal areas in equal times.
• The square of a planet's orbital period is proportional to the cube of its semi-major axis, or half the long axis of the orbit.

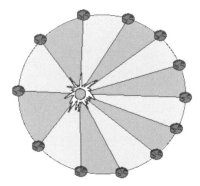

An imaginary line drawn from the Sun to any planet sweeps out equal areas in equal amounts of time.

LAST WORDS OF THE FAMOUS AND THE BRAVE

Take away those pillows. I shall need them no more.
LEWIS CARROLL (1832–98)

Oh, is that all there is?
EMILY DICKINSON (1830–86)
(on being offered a glass of water)

A dying man can do nothing easy.
BENJAMIN FRANKLIN (1706–90)

I am quite happy. Unaccountably happy.
ALLEN GINSBERG (1926–97)

I think it's time for morphine.
D.H. LAWRENCE (1885–1930)

I am just going outside and I may be some time.
CAPTAIN LAWRENCE OATES (1880–1912)

Lord help my poor soul.
EDGAR ALLAN POE (1809–49)

Please put out the light.
THEODORE ROOSEVELT (1858–1919)

Had we lived, I should have had a tale to tell of the hardihood, endurance, and courage of my companions, which would have stirred the hearts of every Englishman. These rough notes and our dead bodies tell the tale.
ROBERT FALCON SCOTT (1868–1912)

I am dying like a poisoned rat in a hole. I am what I am!
JONATHAN SWIFT (1667–1745)

I feel here that this time they have succeeded.
LEON TROTSKY (1879–1940)

Don't let it end like this. Tell them I said something.
PANCHO VILLA (1878–1923)

THE FLAG OF VATICAN CITY

A square flag divided into two equal vertical bands of color. On the right, yellow; on the left, white. On the white area is surmounted the Papal crown and two crossed keys, which represent the keys to the Kingdom of Heaven.

WIND FORCES

Wind strength is measured
by the Beaufort Scale,
devised by Sir Francis
Beaufort (1774–1857)
while he was commander
of HMS *Woolwich* in 1805.
Beaufort's original scale ran
from 0 to 13, but he later
simplified it. The scale came into common
use after its adoption by the British Admiralty in 1838.

0 Calm: Windspeed less than 1 knot/ 0.5m/s*
1 Light air: Windspeed less than 3 knots/ 1.5m/s
2 Light breeze: Windspeed less than 6 knots/ 3.3m/s
3 Gentle breeze: Windspeed less than 10 knots/ 5.4m/s
4 Moderate breeze: Windspeed less than 16 knots/ 7.9m/s
5 Fresh breeze: Windspeed less than 21 knots/ 10.7m/s
6 Strong breeze: Windspeed less than 27 knots/ 13.8m/s
7 Near gale: Windspeed less than 33 knots/ 17.1m/s
8 Gale: Windspeed less than 40 knots/ 20.7m/s
9 Strong gale: Windspeed less than 47 knots/ 24.4m/s
10 Storm: Windspeed less than 55 knots/ 28.4m/s
11 Violent storm: Windspeed less than 63 knots/ 32.6m/s
12 Hurricane: Windspeed over 64 knots/ 32.7m/s

* 1 knot = 1.15 mph; m/s = meters per second

THE FLAG OF LIECHTENSTEIN

The top half is blue, with a yellow coronet in the top corner on the
hoist side. The bottom half is red. The coronet was added after the
1936 Olympic Games, where it was discovered that the flag of Haiti was
otherwise almost identical.

PUNISHMENT, ROMAN STYLE

Broadly speaking, it was better to be higher up the social ladder when it came to punishment, Roman style. Decapitation was the execution of choice for nobility because it was quick. Favorite methods of execution were:

- Crucifixion: most often preceded by scourging, a series of violent blows with a whip made of leather and metal.
- Death by animal mutilation: thrown to the lions, leopards, or wild boars; considered fitting for people of a servile status.
- Death by burning.

Although these were the norm, different emperors had their own cruel punishments:

Augustus (63 BC–AD 14): broke the legs of his secretary for betraying the contents of a letter.

Constantine (?280–337): those aiding the abduction of a virgin had molten lead poured down their throats.

Galba (3 BC–AD 69): punished a money lender by amputating his hands and nailing him to his table.

Nero (37–68): executed Christians as arsonists after the fire of AD 64 by covering them in pitch and setting fire to their bodies to illuminate the evening's entertainment.

SONGS ABOUT ROADS

Song	Artist
Baker Street	Gerry Rafferty
Country Road	John Denver
Every Day is a Winding Road	Sheryl Crow
Goodbye Yellow Brick Road	Elton John
Highway 61 Revisited	Bob Dylan
King of the Road	Roger Miller
The Long and Winding Road	The Beatles
Route 66	Bobby Troupe
Why Don't We Do It in the Road	The Beatles

THE PILOT'S ALPHABET

First developed by NATO in the 1940s to unify the various radio
alphabets used by the Allies in World War II, this alphabet is now widely
used in international aviation and any situation where clear radio
communication (often between non-native English speakers)
is needed.

Alpha
Bravo
Charlie
Delta
Echo
Foxtrot
Golf
Hotel
India
Juliet
Kilo
Lima
Mike
November
Oscar
Papa
Quebec
Romeo
Sierra
Tango
Uniform
Victor
Whisky
X-Ray
Yankee
Zulu

The composition of palindromes (words or phrases that are the same whether read backward or forward has been one of the most popular word games since antiquity. In fact, the word originates with the Greek *palindromos* ("running back again"). One of history's most apposite palindromes was allegedly penned by Napoleon Bonaparte after his defeat and exile to the island of Elba—"Able was I ere I saw Elba." History does not record why the Anglophobic emperor might have been moved to compose in English . . .

Ah, Satan sees Natasha

Do geese see God?

Madam, in Eden, I'm Adam

A man, a plan, a canal—Panama!

I prefer pi

Dammit, I'm mad

Eva, can I stab bats in a cave?

Dennis and Edna sinned

Lager, sir, is regal

Lee had a heel

Senile felines

Devil never even lived

Solo gigolos

Ten animals I slam in a net

Top spot

Was it a rat I saw?

Draw noses onward!

We panic in a pew

Yawn a more Roman way

Gary knits a stinky rag

Cigar? Toss it in a can. It is so tragic

Ed is a trader; cast sacred art aside

Go hang a salami; I'm a lasagna hog

I, man, am regal; a German am I

Campus motto: Bottoms up, Mac

Dennis, Nell, Edna, Leon, Nedra, Anita, Rolf, Nora, Alice, Carol, Leo, Jane, Reed, Dena, Dale, Basil, Rae, Penny, Lana, Dave, Denny, Lena, Ida, Bernadette, Ben, Ray, Lila, Nina, Jo, Ira, Mara, Sara, Mario, Jan, Ina, Lily, Arne, Bette, Dan, Reba, Diane, Lynn, Ed, Eva, Dana, Lynne, Pearl, Isabel, Ada, Ned, Dee, Rena, Joel, Lora, Cecil, Aaron, Flora, Tina, Arden, Noel, and Ellen sinned

HUMOROUS QUOTATIONS

I'm not afraid to die. I just don't want to be there when it happens.
WOODY ALLEN (1935–)

Mothers are fonder than fathers of their children because they are more certain they are their own.
ARISTOTLE (384–322 BC)

Let us have some wine and women, mirth and laughter. Sermons and soda-water the day after.
LORD BYRON (1788–1824)

I'm living so far beyond my income that we may almost be said to be living apart.
E E CUMMINGS (1894–1962)

It destroys one's nerves to be amiable every day to the same human being.
BENJAMIN DISRAELI (1804–81)

A woman drove me to drink and I never even had the courtesy to thank her.
W.C. FIELDS (1880–1946)

One dies only once and it's for such a long time!
MOLIÈRE (1622–73)

Even if you're on the right track, you'll get run over if you just sit there.
WILL ROGERS (1879–1935)

Do you know what a pessimist is? A man who thinks everybody is as nasty as himself and hates them for it.
GEORGE BERNARD SHAW (1856–1950)

If you don't take care of your body, where will you live?
UNKNOWN

FOUR HORSEMEN OF THE APOCALYPSE

DEATH	pale horse
FAMINE	black horse
SLAUGHTER	red horse
WAR	white horse

Patron Saints

There are patron saints for most things that might affect our lives: places, feelings, and even parts of the body. Patron saints were once chosen by the pope but now can be chosen by groups or individuals to oversee a particular cause or concern.

Saint	*Patronage*
Matthew	Accountants
Vitus	Actors
Pelagia	Actresses
Francis of Assisi	Animals
Philomena	Babies
Ambrose	Bee keepers
Louis	Button makers
Bridgid of Ireland	Chicken farmers
Genesius	Clowns
Clotilde	Disappointing children
John the Apostle	Friendships
Joseph of Arimathea	Funeral directors
Sebastian	Gardeners
Eligius (Eloi)	Gas station workers
Clare of Assissi	Good weather
Anne	Grandparents
Anthony of Padua	Mail
Agatha	Natural disasters
Nicholas of Myra	Newlyweds
John Nepomucene	Silence
Thomas Aquinas	Students
Claude de la Columbiere	Toy makers
Francis de Sales	Writers

THE WALTZ

The Waltz is unique in that it is the only ballroom dance written in 3/4 time. There are three beats to each measure, counted as "1–2–3" or "quick-quick-quick." Typically, there are three steps of equal duration per measure, with the Hesitation being the exception. The lead foot alternates with each measure (i.e. Left–2–3–Right–2–3). Because of this, Waltz combinations are usually written in a series of six steps. For example, the man will begin the first pattern as LRL (left–right–left) and the second as RLR (right–left–right), for a total of six steps.

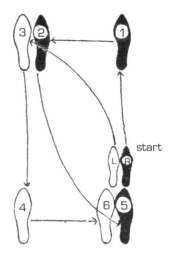

THE PLAGUES OF EGYPT

1 The Nile and other Egyptian waterways turned to blood
2 Frogs
3 Lice (or maggots)
4 Flies
5 Death of livestock
6 Boils
7 Hail
8 Locusts
9 Darkness
10 The slaying of Egyptian firstborn

ORIGINS OF MONTHS

The English names for the months of the year all have their origins in the names that the Romans used.

Name	Derived from	Meaning
January	*Janus*	Roman god (of doorways/bridges) whose two faces look in opposite directions: back over the past year and forward to the new one.
February	*Februa*	Named for a Sabine purification festival, held on February 15, that was adopted by the Romans.
March	*Martius*	The month of Mars, the god of war.
April	*Apru*	The Etruscan word for the Greek goddess of love, Aphrodite.
May	*Maius*	The month of Maia, divine wife of the god Vulcan.
June	*Juno*	Named for Jupiter's wife.
July	*Julius*	Named in honor of Julius Caesar.
August	*Augustus*	Named for Caesar's adopted son and heir, Octavian, after he was granted the title of Augustus.
September	*Septem*	With the seventh month (the Roman year started in March), the Romans ran out of inspiration. *Septem* means "seven."
October	*Octo*	The Latin for "eight."
November	*Novem*	(You've guessed it) "nine."
December	*Decem*	The Latin for "ten."

NATIONAL SPELLING BEE WINNERS

This annual spelling contest, which is sponsored by a number of newspapers, was established in 1925 as a way to encourage children to learn how to spell. Girls and boys from schools around the country compete to enter the national competition held in Washington. Here are the winners and their winning words since 1950:

Year	Champion	Word
1950	Colquitt Dean, Atlanta, GA	meticulosity
1951	Irving Belz, Memphis, TN	insouciant
1952	Doris Ann Hall, Winston-Salem, NC	vignette
1953	Elizabeth Hess, Phoenix, AZ	soubrette
1954	William Cashore, Norristown, PA	transept
1955	Sandra Sloss, St. Louis, MO	crustaceology
1956	Melody Sachko, Pittsburgh, PA	condominium
1957	Sandra Owen, Canton, OH	schappe
	Dana Bennett, Denver, CO	schappe
1958	Jolitta Schlehuber, Topeka, KS	syllepsis
	Joel Montgomery, Denver, CP	catamaran
1959	Hnery Feldman, Knoxville, TN	eudaemonic
1960	John Capehart, Tulsa, OK	smaragdine
1962	Nettie Crawford, El Paso, TX	esquamulose
	Michael Day, St. Louis, MO	esquamulose
1963	Glen Van Slyke III, Knoxville, TN	equipage
1964	William Kerek, Akron, OH	sycophant
1965	Michael Kerpan Jr., Tulsa, OK	eczema
1966	Robert A. Wake, Houston, TX	ratoon
1967	Jennifer Reinke, Omaha, NE	chihuahua
1968	Robert L. Walters, Topeka, KS	abalone
1969	Susan Yoachum, Dallas, TX	interlocutory
1970	Libby Childress, Winston-Salem, NC	croissant
1971	Jonathan Knisely, Philadelphia, PA	shalloon
1972	Robin Kral, Lubbock, TX	macerate

Year	Champion	Word
Year	*Champion*	*Word*
1973	Barrie Trinkle, Fort Worth TX	vouchsafe
1974	Julie Ann Junkin, Birmingham, AL	hydrophyte
1975	Hugh Tosteson, San Juan, PR	incisor
1976	Tim Kneale, Syracuse, NY	nacrolepsy
1977	John Paola, Pittsburgh, PA	cambist
1978	Peg McCarthy, Topeka, KS	deification
1979	Katie Kerwin, Denver, CO	maculature
1980	Jacques Bailly, Denver, CO	elucubrate
1981	Paige Pipkin, El Paso, TX	sarcophagus
1982	Molly Dieveney, Denver, CO	psoriasis
1983	Blake Giddens, El Paso, TX	Purim
1984	Daniel Greenblatt, Leesburg, VA	luge
1985	Balu Natarajan, Chicago, IL	milieu
1986	Jon Pennington, Harrisburg, PA	odontalgia
1987	Stephanie Petit, Pittsburgh, PA	staphylococci
1988	Rageshree Ramachandran, Sacramento, CA	elegiacal
1989	Scott Isaacs, Denver, CO	spoliator
1990	Amy Marie Dimak, Seattle, WA	fibranne
1991	Joanne Lagatta, Madison, WI	antipyretic
1992	Amanda Goad, Richmond, VA	lyceum
1993	Geoff Hooper, Memphis, TN	kamikaze
1994	Ned G. Andrews, Knoxville, TN	antediluvian
1995	Justin Tyler Carroll, Memphis, TN	xanthosis
1996	Wendy Guey, West Palm Beach, FL	vivisepulture
1997	Rebecca Sealfon, New York, NY	euonym
1998	Jody-Anne Maxwell, Kingston, Jamaica	chiaroscurist
1999	Nupur Lala, Tampa, FL	logorrhea
2000	George Abraham Thampy, St. Louis, MO	demarche
2001	Sean Conley, Aikin, MN	succedaneum
2002	Pratyush Buddiga, Denver, CO	prospicience
2003	Sai R. Gunturi, Dallas, TX	pocourante

FIGURES OF SPEECH

Anaphora

The repetition of a word or phrase (often at the start of successive sentences): e.g. "We shall fight on the beaches. We shall fight on the landing grounds. We shall fight in the fields . . ."

Hyperbole

Deliberate overstatement for dramatic effect: e.g. "He could flatten a building with his left hook."

Litotes

The practice of praising or criticizing something by denying its opposite: e.g. "He's no slouch" or "Her new painting is hardly a Monet."

Metaphor

In a metaphor, a word or description which literally applies to one object is used to refer to another object without making a comparison between the two, as in a simile: e.g. "He is a lion in battle" is a metaphor, while "He is like a lion" is a simile.

Metonymy

The use of a literal term for one thing to reflect a larger, related concept: e.g. "the Stage" to refer to the acting profession, or "Shakespeare" to refer to his works.

Oxymoron

The combination of two, usually contradictory terms in one word or phrase: e.g. "Parting is such sweet sorrow."

Periphrasis

A roundabout way of saying something without directly referring to it: e.g. "He's passed away" istead of "He's dead."

Personification

The practice of referring to inanimate objects, animals, or abstract concepts as if they were human: e.g. "Mother Nature."

Simile

An overt comparison between two objects, emotions, or actions that uses the words "as" or "like" to form the comparison: e.g. "O my love is like a red, red rose."

Synecdoche

The substitution of part of an object to refer to the whole: e.g. "one hundred sails" to mean "one hundred ships."

FAMOUS LEFT-HANDERS

Aristotle	Helen Keller
Cecil Beaton	John McEnroe
Napolean Bonaparte	Steve McQueen
George H.W. Bush	George Michael
Charlie Chaplin	Michelangelo
Kurt Cobain	Arnold Palmer
Tom Cruise	Robert Redford
Cary Grant	Dr. Albert Schweitzer
Jimi Hendrix	Mark Twain

THE KNIGHT'S VIRTUES

Charity	Prudence
Diligence	Resolution
Faith	Sagacity
Hope	Temperance
Justice	Truth
Liberality	Valor

UNIVERSAL GRAVITATION (1687)

The gravitational force experienced between two objects is proportional to the product of their masses, divided by the square of the distance between them.

THE CURSUS HONORUM

The *cursus honorum* was the hierarchy of Roman offices. After military service, men could begin their climb up the ladder, but there was no skipping of rungs on the way up. The positions were defined rigidly but were marginally different for the different classes (both patrician and plebeian).

→ *7. Dictator*

→ *6. Censor*

→ *5. Consul* Chief magistrates who presided over the Senate and assemblies.

→ *4. Praetor* Primarily judges.

→ *3. Curule aedile* (patricians) or *plebeian aedile* Supervised public places and games.

→ *2. Tribunes* Always plebeian, they could veto acts, convene the Senate and initiate legislation.

→ *1. Quaestor* Administered state finances and eligible for membership; in the Senate.

A FEW WEDDING DO'S AND DON'TS

• If you are sent an invitation, you should buy a gift—whether or not you attend the wedding.
• Never bring someone else to a wedding unless their name is also on the wedding invitation.
• Never wear anything that will compete with the bride. In particular, don't wear black leather or sequins for a morning wedding, or a see-through blouse at any time of day.
• Arrive on time for the ceremony. If an usher offers you his arm, let him lead you to your seat—your guest should walk behind you.

THE CAR'S THE STAR

The cars that have appeared on these well-loved programs have become just as much a part of television history as the characters who drove them.

The Show	The Character	The Car
The Avengers	Emma Peel	Lotus Elan
The Avengers	John Steed	Bentley
Columbo	Columbo	c.1959 Peugeot 403 convertible
The Dukes of Hazzard	Bo and Luke Hazzard	1969 Dodge Charger (The General Lee)
Inspector Morse	Morse	c.1960 Jaguar MKII
Knight Rider	Michael Knight	c.1982 Pontiac Trans-Am (K.I.T.T.)
Starsky & Hutch	Dave Starsky	1976 Ford Gran Torino

YALE SECRET SOCIETIES

Skull and Bones, founded in 1832, is the oldest and most famous of Yale's secret societies. "Bonesmen" are sworn to secrecy, but rumor has it that the society's list of former members includes former presidents Rutherford B. Hayes, William Howard Taft, and George H.W. Bush. President George W. Bush was also part of this exclusive club.

Traditionally, societies choose their new members on Tap Night, in April. After being invited to join the societies, the new members (or "taps") are led, blindfolded, to the society "tomb." Skull and Bones members have secret names, some traditional, some passed on from one Bonesman to another, and others that the new members choose themselves. George W. Bush's "secret" name was Temporary.

Other Yale secret societies are:
• Berzelius and Wolf's Head
• Book and Snake, Scroll and Key
• Society of St Anthony Hall.

PHILOSOPHY, IN BRIEF

Analytic philosophy   An empirical and logically rigorous philosophy widespread in the 20th century, avoiding metaphysical questions in favor of hard-edged analysis.

Cartesianism   A popular 17th-century school, following René Descartes, based on extreme scepticism of the evidence of the senses and a belief that one could only find out about the world by rational deduction.

Cynicism   Ancient Greek school emphasizing stern morality and asceticism, and scorning pleasure and enjoyment.

Deism   Belief in natural laws established by a noninterventionist God, giving rise to a religious duty to be virtuous—highly influential on the founders of the USA.

Determinism   A belief in cause and effect taken to its ultimate conclusion that everything that happens is predetermined.

Empiricism   A belief that all knowledge must be based on experience, supported by John Locke (1632–1704), David Hume (1711–76), and others.

Epicureanism   An ancient Greek school emphasizing pleasure as the basis of an ethical life, and promoting the pleasures of the mind over those of the body.

Existentialism   A belief that human beings have free will and exist in a meaningless Universe; hence, only they can be the judges of their own actions.

Hedonism   A belief that pleasure is the main purpose of life, taken to its ultimate extreme by the Cyrenaic school of ancient Greece.

Humanism   A belief in the importance of human beings above God or religious issues.

Instrumentalism   A belief that the value of theories and ideas is measured by the success of their predictions and explanations.

Logical atomism An approach to philosophy involving breaking down arguments into their simplest propositions.

Logical positivism A belief that philosophy must take a scientific approach, and that its success can only be judged empirically.

Materialism A belief that there is nothing beyond the material Universe, and that mind is simply a feature of matter.

Platonism The teachings of Plato (*c.*428–348 BC) and his followers, who rejected the material world as an imperfect reflection of perfect forms that can only be appreciated and understood by logic and deduction.

Pragmatism A school measuring the value of philosophical beliefs by the usefulness of the effects.

Rationalism A belief that all knowledge must be deduced logically from first principles— the opposite of empiricism.

Reductionism The practice of explanation by reducing things to their smallest parts.

Scepticism Belief that obtaining absolute knowledge of anything is ultimately impossible.

Socratic method The principles of logical argument promoted by Socrates (*c.*470–399 BC), who was concerned with countering the sceptical beliefs of the Sophist school, and proving that it was possible to find absolute truths.

Stoicism An ancient Greek school emphasizing submission to the laws of the Universe as the path to happiness.

Utilitarianism The theory that an action's ethical value should be judged by its outcome.

> *The point of philosophy is to start with something so simple as to seem not worth stating, and to end with something so paradoxical that no one will believe it.*
> BERTRAND RUSSELL (1872–1970)

WHERE IN THE (STAR WARS) WORLD?

Episode IV—A New Hope (1977):
Tatooine, the Death Star, the fourth moon of Yavin

Episode V—The Empire Strikes Back (1980):
Hoth, the asteroid belt, Dagobah, Bespin

Episode VI: Return of the Jedi (1983):
Tatooine, Dagobah, Endor, the Death Star (Mk II)

Episode I: The Phantom Menace (1999):
Naboo, Tatooine, Coruscant

Episode II: Attack of the Clones (2002):
Coruscant, Naboo , Kamino, Geonosis, Tatooine

Episode III . . . the story continues in 2005.

USEFUL MATHEMATICAL FORMULAE

Circumference of a circle = $2\pi r$

Area of a circle = πr^2

Volume of a sphere = $\frac{4}{3} \pi r^3$

Volume of a cylinder = $\pi r^2 h$

Volume of a cone base = $\frac{1}{3} \pi r^2 h$

(*Note:* r = radius, h = height, π [pi] = 3.14159 265)

LINNAEN ORDER OF CLASSIFICATION

KINGDOM *subkingdom*

  PHYLUM *subphylum*

    PHYLUM *subphylum superclass*

      CLASS *subclass infraclass cohort superorder*

        ORDER *suborder superfamily*

          FAMILY *subfamily tribe*

            GENUS *subgenus*

              SPECIES *subspecies*

THIS BOOK IS DEDICATED TO . . .

Book	Author	Dedication
Carrie	Stephen King	This is for Tabby, who got me into it—and then bailed me out of it.
Faking It	Jennifer Crusie	For PAT GAFFNEY for her magnificent novels, limitless patience, and unconditional friendship, and because she totally gets the *Buffy the Vampire Slayer* thing.
Goodbye Harold, (Good Luck)	Audrey Thomas	To Claire, who doesn't laugh (too hard) when I look for the iron in the fridge.
I Like It Like That	Claire Calman	F R L R E O A R V H W Y O L T I What took you so long?
Skinny Legs and All	Tom Robbins	For Alexa d'Avalon and Ginny Ruffner and their pink shoes.
The War of Don Emmanuel's Nether Parts	Louis de Bernières	To the Incorrigible and Legendary Don Benjamin of Poponte, who entrusted me with several children and three horses.
This Way Up	Holly Fox	For Mom, in loving memory of the levitating donkey, a chimney brush in the next street, and the fresh egg wars.

WORLD SERIES WINNERS

American League teams have won 58 times, National League teams, 40 times. Here's a list of the winners.

Team	Number of wins	Years won
New York Yankees	26	1923, '27, '28, '32, '36, '37, '38, '39, '41, '43, '47, '49, '50, '51, '52, '53, '56, '58, '61, '62, '77, '78, '96, '98, '99, 2000
St. Louis Cardinals	9	1926, '31, '34, '42, '44, '46, '64, '67, '82
Boston Red Sox	5	1903, '12, '15, '16, '18
Cincinnati Reds	5	1919, '40, '75, '76, '90
Los Angeles Dodgers	5	1959, '63, '65, '81, '88
New York Giants	5	1905, '21, '22, '33, '54
Philadelphia Athletics	5	1910, '11, '13, '29, '30
Pittsburgh Pirates	5	1909, '25, '60, '71, '79
Detroit Tigers	4	1935, '45, '68, '84
Oakland Athletics	4	1972, '73, '74, '89
Baltimore Orioles	3	1966, '70, '83
Chicago Cubs	2	1907, '08
Chicago White Sox	2	1906, '17
Cleveland Indians	2	1920, '48
Florida Marlins	2	1997, 2003
Minnesota Twins	2	1987, '91
New York Mets	2	1969, '86
Toronto Blue Jays	2	1992, '93
Anaheim Angels	1	2002
Arizona Diamondbacks	1	2001
Atlanta Braves	1	1995
Boston Braves	1	1914
Brooklyn Dodgers	1	1955
Milwaukee Braves	1	1957
Philadelphia Phillies	1	1980
Kansas City Royals	1	1985
Washington Senators	1	1924

In the Time of Ptolemy (305–30 BC)

Life in Eygpt during the Ptolemaic period was confusing. In this dynasty all the pharoahs have the same name—Ptolemy—they frequently married their sisters and sometimes, their mothers.

Ptolemy I: Name not known, but daughter of Nectanebo;
Q. Eurydice (Macedonian); Q. Berenice
Ptolemy II: Q. Arsinoe I (from Thrace); Q. Arsinoe II
(also his sister)
Ptolemy III: Q. Berenice (Cyrenian)
Ptolemy IV: Q. Arsinoe (also his sister)
Ptolemy V: Q. Cleopatra I
Ptolemy VI: Q. Cleopatra II
Ptolemy VII (killed by Ptolemy VIII as soon as he
had an heir)
Ptolemy VIII: Q. Cleopatra II (also his sister); Q. Cleopatra III
(daughter of Cleopatra II and his niece)
Ptolemy X: Q. Cleopatra III (also his mother who took him
as consort because he was her favorite)
Ptolemy IX (reclaimed the throne after his brother, Ptolemy X,
was killed): Q. Cleopatra IV
Ptolemy XI: Q. Berenice (also his aunt and the legitimate
heir to Ptolemy IX)
Ptolemy XII: Q. Tryphaena
(also his sister); Q. Berenice IV
Ptolemy XIII: Q. Cleopatra VII
(rightful heir, forced to marry
her brother)
Ptolemy XIV: Q. Cleopatra VII
(again, rightful heir, marries
another brother, becomes
Caesar's mistress, and bears
him Ptolemy XV [Caesarion])

OSCAR WINNERS: BEST FILM

Title	Director	Date
Wings	William A. Wellman	1928
The Broadway Melody	Harry Beaumont	1929
All Quiet on the Western Front	Lewis Milestone	1930
Cimarron	Wesley Ruggles	1931
Grand Hotel	Edmund Goulding	1932
Cavalcade	Frank Lloyd	1933
It Happened One Night	Frank Capra	1934
Mutiny on the Bounty	Frank Lloyd	1935
The Great Zeigfield	Robert Z. Leonard	1936
The Life of Emile Zola	William Dieterle	1937
You Can't Take It With You	Frank Capra	1938
Gone With the Wind	Victor Fleming	1939
Rebecca	Alfred Hitchcock	1940
How Green Was My Valley	John Ford	1941
Mrs. Miniver	William Wyler	1942
Casablanca	Michael Curtiz	1943
Going My Way	Leo McCarey	1944
The Lost Weekend	Billy Wilder	1945
The Best Years of Our Lives	William Wyler	1946
Gentlemen's Agreement	Elia Kazan	1947
Hamlet	Laurence Olivier	1948
All the King's Men	Robert Rossen	1949
All About Eve	Joseph L Mankiewicz	1950
An American in Paris	Vincente Minnelli	1951
The Greatest Show on Earth	Cecil B DeMille	1952
From Here to Eternity	Fred Zinnemann	1953
On the Waterfront	Elia Kazan	1954
Marty	Delbert Mann	1955
Around the World in 80 Days	Michael Anderson	1956
The Bridge on the River Kwai	David Lean	1957
Gigi	Vincente Minnelli	1958
Ben-Hur	William Wyler	1959
The Apartment	Billy Wilder	1960
West Side Story	J. Robbins & R. Wise	1961
Lawrence of Arabia	David Lean	1962
Tom Jones	Tony Richardson	1963
My Fair Lady	George Cukor	1964

The Sound of Music	Robert Wise	1965
A Man For All Seasons	Fred Zinnemann	1966
In the Heat of the Night	Norman Jewison	1967
Oliver!	Carol Reed	1968
Midnight Cowboy	John Schlesinger	1969
Patton	Franklin J. Schaffner	1970
The French Connection	William Friedkin	1971
The Godfather	Francis Ford Coppola	1972
The Sting	George Roy Hill	1973
The Godfather Part II	Francis Ford Coppola	1974
One Flew Over the Cuckoo's Nest	Milos Forman	1975
Rocky	John G. Avildsen	1976
Annie Hall	Woody Allen	1977
The Deer Hunter	Michael Cimino	1978
Kramer vs Kramer	Robert Benton	1979
Ordinary People	Robert Redford	1980
Chariots of Fire	Hugh Hudson	1981
Ghandi	Richard Attenborough	1982
Terms of Endearment	James L. Brooks	1983
Amadeus	Milos Forman	1984
Out of Africa	Sydney Pollack	1985
Platoon	Oliver Stone	1986
The Last Emperor	Bernardo Bertolucci	1987
Rain Man	Barry Levinson	1988
Driving Miss Daisy	Bruce Beresford	1989
Dances With Wolves	Kevin Costner	1990
The Silence of the Lambs	Jonathan Demme	1991
Unforgiven	Clint Eastwood	1992
Schindler's List	Steven Spielberg	1993
Forrest Gump	Robert Zemeckis	1994
Braveheart	Mel Gibson	1995
The English Patient	Anthony Minghella	1996
Titanic	James Cameron	1997
Shakespeare in Love	John Madden	1998
American Beauty	Sam Mendes	1999
Gladiator	Ridley Scott	2000
A Beautiful Mind	Ron Howard	2001
Chicago	Rob Marshall	2002
The Lord of the Rings: Return of the King	Peter Jackson	2003

THE PLANETS

	Average distance from Sun: miles (km) (million)	Length of year	Rotation period (i.e. one day)	Equatorial diameter: miles (km)	Mass (Earth = 1)
Mercury	36 (57.9)	87.97 days	58.65 days	3,031 (4,880)	0.0553
Venus	67.2 (108.2)	224.70 days	243.01 days	7,518 (12,104)	0.815
Earth	92.9 (149.6)	365.26 days	23.934 hours	7,923 (12,756)	1
Mars	141.6 (227.9)	686.98 days	24.623 hours	4,219 (6,792)	0.1074
Jupiter	486.4 (778.3)	11.86 Earth years	9.842 hours	88,810 (142,984)	317.71
Saturn	886.3 (1,427)	29.46 Earth years	10.233 hours	74,867 (120,536)	95.162
Uranus	1,783 (2,870)	84.01 Earth years	17.240 hours	31,750 (51,118)	14.535
Neptune	2,793 (4,497)	164.79 Earth years	16.110 hours	30,765 (49,532)	17.141
Pluto	3,700 (5,900)	248.50 Earth years	6.387 days	1,429 (2,300)	0.002

The body of Benjamin Franklin Printer
(like the cover of an old book
Its contents worn out
And stripped of its lettering and golding)
Lies here, food for the worms,
Yet the work shall not be lost,
For it shall (as he believed) appear once more
In a new and most beautiful edition
Corrected and Revised
By the Author.
Boston, Massachusetts, USA

Here lies my wife
Here lies she
Hellelujah!
Hallelujee!
Leeds, England

It was a cough that carried him off
It was a coffin they carried him off in.
Massachusetts, USA

Here lies John Yeast
Pardon me for not rising.
New Mexico, USA

Here lies the body of Martha Dias
Who was always uneasy and not over-pious
She lived to the age of three score and ten
And gave to the worms what she refused to the men.
Shrewsbury, England

GOLD STANDARDS

Gold is graded in carats, a measure of its purity or fineness, measured in parts pure gold out of 24. Hence 24-carat gold is the purest, softest, and most golden-colored. Other grades of gold are as follows:

22 carat—91.6% pure
20 carat—85% pure
18 carat—75% pure
14 carat—58.5% pure
10 carat—41.6% pure
9 carat—37.5% pure

Gold is most commonly alloyed with copper or silver, and becomes progressively harder and less golden in color with decreasing purity (although this also depends on the other metals in the alloy). Common alloys are:

9-ct Yellow: 10% silver, 45% copper, 7.5% zinc
9-ct White:*   0% silver, 40% copper, 10.4% zinc, 11.8% nickel,
                        or palladium
14-ct Yellow: 4% silver, 31.2% copper, 6.3% zinc
14-ct White: 0.5% silver, 27% copper, 7% zinc, 7% nickel,
                        or palladium
18-ct Yellow: 16% silver, 9% copper
18-ct White: 4% silver, 4% copper, 17% palladium
22-ct Yellow:*   5.5% silver, 2.8% copper

*Gold makes up the rest of the alloy to 100%.

DISTANCE CONVERSION TABLE

miles (m)	m or km	kilometers (km)	miles (m)	m or km	kilometers (km)
0.621	1	1.609	3.728	6	9.656
1.243	2	3.219	4.350	7	11.265
1.864	3	4.828	4.971	8	12.874
2.486	4	6.437	5.593	9	14.484
3.107	5	8.047	6.214	10	16.093

CAPITAL CITIES

Country	Capital	Country	Capital
Afghanistan	Kabul	Jamaica	Kingston
Albania	Tirana	Jordan	Amman
Bermuda	Hamilton	Lebanon	Beirut
Bolivia	Sucre	Malta	Valletta
Bosnia-Herzegovina	Sarajevo	Monaco	Monaco-
Canada	Ottawa		Ville
Chile	Santiago	Myanmar (Burma)	Yangon
Colombia	Bogotá	Nepal	Katmandu
Croatia	Zagreb	Nicaragua	Managua
Cyprus	Nicosia	Slovakia	Bratislava
Czech Republic	Prague	Sri Lanka	Colombo
Estonia	Tallinn	Taiwan	Taipei
Fiji	Suva	Tanzania	Dodoma
Gambia	Banjul	Uruguay	Montevideo
Ghana	Accra	Venezuela	Caracas

LENGTH OF PREGNANCY IN VARIOUS MAMMALS

Animal	Length of pregnancy	Blind/not blind at birth
African elephant	21–25 months	Not blind
American opossum	12–13 days	Blind
Blue whale	11–12 months	Not blind
Domestic dog	8–9 weeks	Blind
Giraffe	14–15 months	Not blind
Golden hamster	16 days	Blind
Human	9 months	Not blind
Rhinoceros	15–18 months	Not blind
Salamander*	up to 38 months	Not blind

*Not a mammal, but one species—the alpine black salamander—has the longest
gestation period of any animal. It gives birth to its two live young after a pregnancy of
up to 38 months. The higher up in the Alps they live, the longer the pregnancy: at
4,600 ft (1,400 m) it is 38 months.

IT'S MAYAN TIME!

The Mayan calendar, which was adopted by many other MesoAmerican civilizations, is remarkable for its complexity. In fact, the Mayans had three ways of measuring the date. Their civil calendar (or Haab) used 18 months of 20 days, followed by a further period of 5 days (called the Uayeb), making a total of 365 days.

The "divinatory calendar" (or Tzolkin) consisted of two methods of counting weeks, running in parallel—days were numbered 1 to 13, and also named in a cycle of 20 names. The sequence repeated every 260 days. The Haab and Tzolkin synchronize every 52 Haab years, and at these times the Maya feared the world might end.

The final element of the Mayan calendar was the "Long Count," representing the number of kin (or days since the beginning of the world). The Long Count measured cycles as follows:

1 uinal	=	20 kin
1 tun	=	18 uinal
1 katun	=	20 tun
1 baktun	=	20 katun

The longest element of the Long Count—the baktun—was equal, therefore, to 144,000 days, or approximately 394.25 years. For reasons best known to themselves, the Mayans started counting at "13.0.0.0.0" (i.e. 13 baktun, 0 katun, 0 tun, 0 uinal, 0 kin), and counted the baktuns down rather than up. The smaller units are then counted upward (according to the relationship in the previous paragraph), but when a cycle of 20 katun is completed, the baktun number is reduced by 1—so you go from "13.19.19.17.19" to "12.0.0.0.0," and so on.

Since the weight of opinion is that the Long Count measured time from August 3114 BC, the Long Count will probably reach zero (i.e. 0.0.0.0.0) in December 2012—a fact that has already inspired a number of books that you can find in the Mind-Body-Spirit section of your local bookstore.

PEN NAMES

TRUMAN CAPOTE (1924–84)
Truman Persons
In Cold Blood

LEWIS CARROLL (1832–98)
Charles Lutwidge Dodgson
Alice in Wonderland

DANTE (1265–1321)
Durante Alighieri
The Divine Comedy

ISAK DINESEN (1885–1962)
Baroness Karen Blixen Finecke
Out of Africa

GEORGE ELIOT
(1819–80)
Mary Ann Evans
Middlemarch

FLANN O'BRIEN (1911–66)

Brian O'Nolan
At Swim-Two-Birds

GEORGE ORWELL (1903–50)
Eric Arthur Blair
Animal Farm

GEORGE SAND (1804–76)
Amandine Aurore Lucie Dupin,
Baronne Dudevant
Horace

MARK TWAIN (1885–1910)
Samuel Langhorne Clemens
Adventures of Huckleberry Finn

REBECCA WEST (1892–1983)
Mrs H.M. Andrews,
née Cicily Fairfield
Black Lamb and Gray Falcon

ROMAN NUMERALS

I	=	1	VIII	=	8	XV	=	15	LXXX =	80
II	=	2	IX	=	9	XX	=	20	XC	=	90
III	=	3	X	=	10	XXX	=	30	C	=	100
IV	=	4	XI	=	11	XL	=	40	D	=	500
V	=	5	XII	=	12	L	=	50	M	=	1,000
VI	=	6	XIII	=	13	LX	=	60	MM	=	2,000
VII	=	7	XIV	=	14	LXX	=	70			

THE SEMAPHORE ALPHABET

Semaphore systems were used by the ancient Greeks and Romans, but came into their own in the 1600s, when the telescope vastly increased their range and efficiency. In 1794 French engineer Claude Chappe designed a mechanized version that used semaphore towers to signal across great distances, but this was soon supplanted by the electric telegraph. Today, the classic colored-flag semaphore system is mostly used for communication between ships without radio contact.

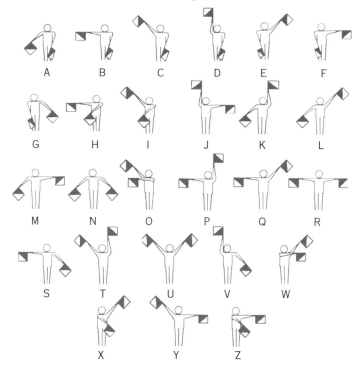

METRIC CONVERSION TABLES

LENGTH

1 inch (in)		= 2.54 centimeters
1 foot (ft)	= 12 inches	= 30.48 centimeters
1 yard (yd)	= 3 feet	= 0.9144 meter
1 mile (mi)	= 1,760 yards	= 1.6093 kilometers
1 millimeter (mm)	= 1,000 micrometers	= 0.0394 inch
1 centimeter (cm)	= 10 millimeters	= 0.3937 inch
1 meter (m)	= 100 centimeters	= 1.0936 yards
1 kilometer (km)	= 1,000 meters	= 0.6214 mile

AREA

1 sq foot	= 144 sq inches	= 0.0929 sq meter
1 sq yard	= 9 sq feet	= 0.8361 sq meter
1 acre (a)	= 4,840 sq yards	= 4,046.9 sq meters
1 sq centimeter	= 100 sq millimeters	= 01.55 sq inches
1 sq meter	= 10,000 sq centimeters	= 1.196 sq yards
1 hectare (ha)	= 10,000 sq meters	= 2.4711 acres
1 sq kilometer	= 100 hectares	= 0.3861 sq mile

CAPACITY

1 pint (pt)	= 4 gills	= 0.5683 liter
1 gallon (gal)	= 8 pints	= 4.5461 liters
1 litre (l)	= 1 cu decimeter	= 0.22 gallon
1 cu yard	= 27 cu feet	= 0.7646 cu meter
1 cu decimeter (dm)	= 1,000 cu centimeters	= 0.0353 cu foot
1 cu meter	= 1,000 cu decimeters	= 1.3080 cu yards

WEIGHT

1 ounce (oz)	= 437.5 grains	= 28.350 grams
1 pound (lb)	= 16 ounces	= 0.4536 kilogram
1 ton (t)	= 2,204 pounds	= 1.0161 tonnes
1 British stone (st)	= 14 pounds	= 6.3504 kilograms
1 British tonne (t)	= 1,000 kilograms	= 0.9842 ton
1gram (g)	= 1,000 milligrams	= 0.0353 ounce
1 kilogram (kg)	= 1,000 grams	= 2.2046 pounds

SIAMESE TWINS

Although births of conjoined twins had been known before, the term "Siamese twins" was first used to describe Chang and Eng Bunker who were born in Siam in 1811. They were joined at the chest and never separated, although they married the sisters Sallie and Adelaide Yates and fathered 21 children between them. They became famous as an attraction for the Barnum and Bailey Circus in the United States and lived there until their deaths in 1874.

Other famous Siamese twins include:

Daisy and Violet Hilton (1908–69)—American vaudeville performers

Masha and Dasha (b. 1950)—born in Russia and the world's oldest non-separated surviving twins

The Foglia twins (b. 1959)—born in Italy and separated at six years old

HOW TO TELL A CROCODILE FROM AN ALLIGATOR

Crocodiles are found worldwide while alligators and caimans are restricted to the Americas. Crocodiles have longer, narrower snouts, and the sharp fourth tooth of the lower jaw is visible when the mouth is closed. Alligators and caimans have a recess in their upper jaw where this tooth slots, out of sight.

THE FLAG OF SENEGAL

The flag of Senegal is divided into three evenly sized vertical bands. From the hoist side, they are green, yellow, and red. In the center of the yellow band is a green, five-pointed star.

NEARBY STARS

Although astronomers have cataloged millions of stars in our Galaxy, they don't know our stellar backyard that well. This is largely because most of our close neighbors in space are very faint and invisible to the naked eye. The following is a list of the most important nearby stars— although it is likely that there are more still to be found.

Name	Constellation	Distance*	Magnitude**
Proxima Centauri ✧	Centaurus	4.2 l.y.	11
Alpha Centauri A ☆	Centaurus	4.3 l.y.	0
Alpha Centauri B ✹	Centaurus	4.3 l.y.	1.3
Barnard's Star ✧	Ophiuchus	6. l.y.	9.5
Wolf 359 ✧	Leo	7.7 l.y.	13.5 (variable)
BD +36°2147 ✧	Ursa Major	8.2 l.y.	7.5
UV Ceti A + B ✧	Cetus	8.4 l.y.	12.5, 13.0 (variables)
Sirius A + B ✲	Canis Major	8.6 l.y.	-1.46, 8.3
Ross 154 ✧	Sagittarius	9.4 l.y.	10.5
Ross 248 ✧	Andromeda	10.4 l.y.	12.3
Epsilon Eridani ☆	Eridanus	10.8 l.y.	3.7

* *Distance is measured in light years (l.y.), the distance light travels in one year, about 5.87 million million miles*

** *Magnitude is a measure of a star's brightness—the higher the number, the fainter the star. Sirius is the brightest star in the sky, and one of a handful with negative magnitudes (-1.46). The faintest stars visible to the naked eye have magnitude 6*

✧   *Red dwarf*

☆   *Yellow/orange sunlike star*

✲   *Blue/white star, white dwarf*

✹   *Orange star*

GREAT PUT DOWNS *(A collection of scornful remarks)*

Mr. Blair is a man of hidden shallows.
HUGO GURDON, *The Daily Telegraph*, on Tony Blair

His ears make him look like a taxicab with both doors open.
HOWARD HUGHES on Clark Gable

*The affair between Margot Asquith and Margot Asquith will live as one
of the prettiest love stories in all literature.*
DOROTHY PARKER on Margot Asquith

The trouble is that when she speaks without thinking she says what she thinks.
NORMAN ST JOHN STEVAS on Margaret Thatcher

*She looks like a cross between an aardvark and an albino rat surmounted by a
platinum-coated horse bun.*
JOHN SIMON on Barbra Streisand

I'll never put Tom Cruise down. He's already kinda short.
DON SIMPSON (producer) on Tom Cruise

I thought nothing of her writing. I considered her a beautiful little knitter.
DAME EDITH SITWELL on Virginia Woolf

*A large shaggy dog just unchained scouring the beaches of the world and baying
at the moon.*
ROBERT LOUIS STEVENSON on Walt Whitman

The only genius with an IQ of 60.
GORE VIDAL on Andy Warhol

The work of a queasy undergraduate scratching his pimples.
VIRGINIA WOOLF on *Ulysses* by James Joyce

US COINS

Denomination	Cent	Nickel	Dime	Quarter	Half Dollar	Dollar	Golden Dollar
Obverse	Lincoln	Jefferson	Roosevelt	Washington	Kennedy	Susan B. Anthony	Sacagawea and infant son
Date of Issue	1909	1938	1946	1932	1964	1979, 1980, 2000	2000
Reverse	Lincoln Memorial	Monticello	Torch, Olive Branch, Oak Branch	Eagle	Presidential Coat of Arms	Apollo 11 Insignia Eagle	Eagle in flight
Date of Issue	1959	1938	1946	1932	1964	1979, 1980, 1999	2000
Composition	Copper-plated Zinc	Cupro-Nickel	Cupro-Nickel	Cupro-Nickel	Cupro-Nickel	Cupro-Nickel	Manganese-Brass
Weight	2.500 g	5.000 g	2.268 g	5.670 g	11.340 g	8.1 g	8.1 g
Diameter	19.05 mm	21.21 mm	17.91 mm	24.26 mm	30.61 mm	26.5 mm	26.5 mm
	0.750 in	0.835 in	0.705 in	0.955 in	1.205 in	1.043 in	1.043 in
Thickness	1.55 mm	1.95 mm	1.35 mm	1.75 mm	2.15 mm	2.00 mm	2.00 mm
Edge	Plain	Plain	Reeded (118 reeds)	Reeded (119 reeds)	Reeded (150 reeds)	Reeded (133 reeds)	Plain

Current US Coinage in circulation 2003

MONOPOLY FROM AROUND THE WORLD

United Kingdom	*France*
Go	Départ
Old Kent Road	Bvd de Belleville
Whitechapel Road	Rue Lecourbe
Income Tax	Impots sur le Revenue
Kings Cross Station	Gare Montparnasse
The Angel Islington	Rue de Vaugirard
Euston Road	Rue de Courcelles
Pentonville Road	Avenue de la République
Jail	Prison
Pall Mall	Bvd de la Villette
Electric Company	Cie de Distribution d'Électricité
Whitehall	Avenue de Neuilly
Northumberland Avenue	Rue de Paradis
Marylebone Station	Gare de Lyon
Bow Street	Avenue Mozart
Marlborough Street	Bvd Saint-Michel
Vine Street	Place Pigalle
Free Parking	Parc Grutuit
Strand	Avenue Matignon
Fleet Street	Bvd Malesherbes
Trafalgar Square	Avenue Henri-Martin
Fenchurch Street Station	Gare du Nord
Leicester Square	Fauborg Saint-Honoré
Coventry Street	Place de la Bourse
Water Works	Cie de Distribution des Eaux
Piccadilly	Rue Lafayette
Go to Jail	Allez en Prison
Regent Street	Avenue de Breteuil
Oxford Street	Avenue Foch
Bond Street	Bvd des Capucines
Liverpool Street Station	Gare Saint-Lazare
Park Lane	Avenue des Champs-Élysées
Super Tax	Taxe de Luxe
Mayfair	Rue de la Paix
Community Chest	Caisse de Communauté
Chance	Chance

Germany		United States of America	
Los		Go	
Badstraße		Mediterranean Avenue	
Turnstraße		Baltic Avenue	
Einkommensteuer		Income Tax	
Südbahnhof		Reading Railroad	
Chausse Straße		Oriental Avenue	
Elisenstraße		Vermont Avenue	
Poststraße		Connecticut Avenue	
Gefängnis		Jail	
Seestraße		St. Charles Place	
Elektrizitäts-Werk		Electric Company	
Häfenstraße		States Avenue	
Neue Straße		Virginia Avenue	
Westbahnhof		Pennsylvania Railroad	
Muchner Straße		St. James Place	
Weiner Straße		Tennessee Avenue	
Berliner Straße		New York Avenue	
Frei Parken		Free Parking	
Theater Straße		Kentucky Avenue	
Museum Straße		Indiana Avenue	
Opernplatz		Illinois Avenue	
Nordbahnhof		B & O Railroad	
Lessing Straße		Atlantic Avenue	
Schiller-Straße		Ventnor Avenue	
Wasser-Werk		Water Works	
Goethe-Straße		Marvin Gardens*	
Gehen Sie in Das Gefängnis		Go to Jail	
Rathaus Platz		Pacific Avenue	
Haupt Straße		North Carolina Avenue	
Bahnhof-Straße		Pennsylvania Avenue	
Haupt Bahnhof		Short Line	
Parkstraße		Park Place	
Zusatzsteuer		Luxury Tax	
Schloballee		Boardwalk	
Gemeinschafts-Feld		Community Chest	
Ereignis-Feld		Chance	

*Should be Marven Gardens, but misprinted in 1932 and deliberately continued today.

THE STRANGE DEATHS OF SOME SAINTS

Many saints were martyrs killed for their Christian beliefs, but some saints met particularly violent and prolonged deaths.

Saint Catherine of Alexandria

Catherine was tied to a wheel set with razors intended to shred her to death, but the wheel broke and Catherine was beheaded.

Saint Cecilia

Sentenced to death by suffocation in her bathroom, Cecilia was unharmed by scalding steam so they tried to behead her. For three days she lay with a badly mutilated neck before finally dying.

Saint Eustace

Eustace, his wife, and two sons were ordered to death in Rome. They were all taken to the Coliseum, encased in a brazen bull, and burned to death.

Saint Herculanus

King Totila ordered that Herculanus had a thin slice of skin pulled off all over his body before being beheaded. In the end, he was executed before all of his body had been tortured.

Saint Jonah

After torture, Jonah was crushed to death in a wine press.

Saint Lawrence

The prefect of Rome heated a large gridiron until it glowed red, bound Lawrence to the metal, and roasted him to death.

Saint Venantius

The 17-year-old saint was burned with flaming torches, hanged upside down over a fire, had his teeth knocked out, and his jaw broken. Then he was thrown to the lions, tossed over a cliff, and, finally, beheaded.

MAKING THE YEARS RUN ON TIME

The modern western calendar was introduced by Pope Gregory XIII in 1582. Keeping the seasons in line with any calendar system of fixed months and days is a problem because the Earth does not complete an orbit of the Sun (and a cycle of seasons) in a whole number of days—instead it takes 365.2422 days. The Gregorian Calendar takes this into account by inserting an extra day every 4 years, but omitting them in centennial years unless the year is exactly divisible by 400 (so 1900 was not a leap year, but 2000 was). This gives an average year length of 265.2425 days, equivalent to just one day lost in 3,300 years.

INUIT WORDS FOR SNOW

Debate rages about how many words the Inuit language has for snow. It certainly has a great variety. Some claim 40, others many fewer. Here are some: **aniugaviniq** hard, frozen snow; **apigiannagaut** the first snowfall of the fall; **katakartanaq** snow with a crust that gives way under the feet; **kinirtaq** compact, damp snow; **mannguq** melting snow; **masak** wet, falling snow; **matsaaq** half-melted snow; **natiruvaaq** drifting snow; **pukak** crystalline snow; **qannialaaq** light-falling snow.

SOME PHARAOHS' WIVES

Wife	Pharaoh	Notable fact
ANKHESENAMEN	Tutankhamun	She was 13 when she married the 8-year-old Tutankhamun
HETEPHESES	Snofru	Mother of Khufu, builder of the Great Pyramid of Giza
NEFERTARI	Ramses II	Buried in one of the most beautiful tombs in the Valley of the Queen
NEFERTITI	Akhenaton	Name means "the beautiful woman has come"
TIY	Amenhotep III	Mother of the "heretic" pharaoh, Akhenaton

THE MOHS SCALE OF HARDNESS

Still used as a way of rating the hardness of materials, the Mohs scale was devised in 1812 by German mineralogist Friedrich Mohs (1773–1839). It places materials on a scale from soft to hard by whether they can or cannot scratch each other. Here is the basic scale:

1	Talc	**6**	Orthoclase
2	Gypsum	**7**	Quartz
3	Calcite	**8**	Topaz
4	Fluorite	**9**	Corundum
5	Apatite	**10**	Diamond

A steel file might measure about 7 on the Mohs scale, window glass about 6, human teeth around 5, and a fingernail between 2 and 3.

CRYPTIC COMMENTS

At a loss for words? Give yourself an air of mystery with one of these cryptic foreign sayings:

If needs must, a pig can be called uncle. (Albanian saying)

Do not try to swat a fly from your friend's forehead using a hatchet. (Chinese)

If your head is made of butter, don't become a baker. (Danish)

No worries? Go and buy a goat. (Indian)

One who is tempted today by a cucumber will be tempted tomorrow by a goat. (Indian)

If you toss cakes at a man, he will toss them back. (Japanese)

SANTA'S ORIGINAL REINDEER

Dasher • Dancer • Prancer • Vixen • Comet •
Cupid • Donner • Blitzen • [Rudolph came later]

ETIQUETTE
"Manners are made up of trivialities of deportment which can be easily learned if one does not happen to know them; manner is personality—the outward manifestation of one's innate character and attitude toward life."

EMILY POST (1872–1960), the doyenne of American etiquette writers

At a formal dinner party
Watch and wait for the hostess to put her napkin on her lap, then follow suit. When you've finished eating, place your used utensils close together on the plate, thus signalling to your servers that the dishes can be removed.

Correspondence
Black ink is the best choice when writing any letters. Blue is in second place, but traditionally thought to be more suitable for women.

Never, ever . . .
... take a drink when your mouth is already filled with food.

... leave your spoon in your cup.

... eat, talk, or wear noisy jewelry during a performance at the theater, opera, or ballet.

... forget to take your hat off in the presence of the dead, in a private house, or a Christian church.

PRESIDENTAL OATH
On first entering the office of President, as specified in Article II, Section 1, of the Constitution, the following oath must be taken:

> "I do solemnly swear (or affirm) that I will faithfully execute the office of President of the United States, and will to the best of my ability, preserve, protect, and defend the Constitution of the United States."

PYTHAGORAS'S THEOREM AND TRIGONOMETRY

In a right-angled triangle, the longest side, is called the hypotenuse. The square of the length of the hypotenuse is equal to the sum of the squares of the other two sides.

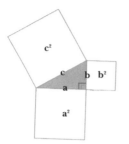

We can write this more simply as:

$$a^2 + b^2 = c^2$$

To work out the angles or lengths of other sides, trigonometry is required. For either of the non-right-angle corners, one side can be called the adjacent and the other the opposite. Trigonometry allows you to work out any angle in the triangle if you know the length of two sides:

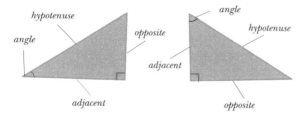

Sin of angle a = opposite length/hypotenuse

Cos a = adjacent/hypotenuse

Tan a = opposite/adjacent

(These ratios can be easily remembered by the schoolroom abbreviation SOHCAHTOA.)

WHAT ASTRONAUTS REALLY EAT*

Intermediate moisture:
Bacon squares
Apricot
Peaches
Brownies (4)
Caramel candy
Chocolate bar
Jellied fruit candy
Beef jerky
Pecans (6)
Pineapple fruitcake
Dehydrated:
Cinnamon toasted bread cubes (4)
Creamed chicken bites (6)
Cheese crackers
Cheese sandwiches (4)
Beef sandwiches (4)
Sugar cookies (4)
Turkey bites (4)
Rehydratable spoon bowl:
Canadian bacon and apple sauce
Cornflakes
Fruit cocktail
Sausage patties
Scrambled eggs
Peaches
Spiced fruit cereal
Apple sauce
Butterscotch pudding
Banana pudding
Chocolate pudding
Cranberry and orange sauce

Peach ambrosia
Chicken and rice soup
Lobster bisque
Pea soup
Potato soup
Shrimp cocktail
Tomato soup
Tuna salad
Beef pot roast
Beef and vegetables
Beef stew
Chicken and rice
Chicken and vegetables
Chicken stew
Pork and scalloped potatoes
Spaghetti with meat sauce
Natural state:
Cubes of crushed peanuts (4)
Sliced bread
Ketchup
2 oz (57 g) Cheddar cheese
Jam
Mustard
Peanut butter
Thermostabilized:
8 oz (227 g) Chicken salad
8 oz (227 g) Ham salad
Beef and gravy
Frankfurters
Meatballs and sauce
Turkey and gravy

* On the Apollo *missions: provides an astronaut with 2,800 calories per day of the week-long mission.*

STORYBOOK DOGS

Name	Breed	Book	Author
Argos	Not known	*The Odyssey*	Homer
Bodger	Bull terrier	*The Incredible Journey*	Sheila Burnford
Buck	Half Shepherd, half St. Bernard	*Call of the Wild*	Jack London
Bullseye	Staffordshire bull terrier	*Oliver Twist*	Charles Dickens
Fluffy	Enormous 3-headed guard dog	*Harry Potter and the Sorcerer's Stone*	J.K. Rowling
Hound of the Baskervilles	(*see below*)*	*Hound of the Baskervilles*	Sir Arthur Conan Doyle
Jip	Not known	*Doctor Dolittle stories*	Hugh Lofting
Lassie	Collie	*Lassie Come Home/ Lassie's Rescue Rangers*	Eric Knight
Nana	Old English sheepdog	*Peter Pan*	J.M. Barrie
Old Yeller	Golden labrador	*Old Yeller*	Fred Gipson
Pongo	Dalmatian	*One Hundred and One Dalmatians*	Dodie Smith
Precious	Toy poodle	*The Silence of the Lambs*	Thomas Harris
Timmy	Border collie	*The Famous Five series*	Enid Blyton
Toto	Cairn terrier	*The Wizard of Oz*	Frank L. Baum

* *It was not a pure Bloodhound and not a pure Mastiff; but it appeared to be a combination of the two—gaunt, savage, and as large as a small lioness.*

STAR TREK SPECIES

Species	Appearance	Character
Bajoran	Ridged nose. Most wear decorative earrings in right ear	Spiritual and peaceful
Betazoids	Physically identical to humans	A peaceful race with highly developed telepathic abilities
Borg	Resemble humans, but are covered with artificial implants	A cybernetic race. They brutally assimilate or destroy anything they come across. All Borg consciousness is connected together in the "Collective"
Cardassians	Bumpy foreheads, topped with a swatch of black hair	Warlike and divisive
Ferengi	Shorter than most humanoids, large earlobes, ridged noses	Greedy and cunning. Completely devoted to making a profit
Klingons	They have ridged foreheads, long hair, often bearded	An aggressive and warlike race, obsessed with maintaining their honor
Romulans	Resemble their distant cousins, the Vulcans	An imperialistic and closed species, not as logical as Vulcans
Vulcans	Taller than most humans, pointed ears, arched eyebrows	Extremely logical, often to the point of appearing dispassionate

THE JAPANESE TEA CEREMONY—THE RULES

The traditional tea ceremony consists of numerous rituals and many Japanese take lessons with a teacher. However, some basic rules apply:

永 Guests must be prompt in arriving

永 Shoes are removed before entering a Japanese home or a teahouse

永 Guests are seated according to their positions in the ceremony

永 The host will sit and exchange greetings with the guests

永 A scroll painting, specially chosen by the host, will be hung in the alcove and should be admired by the guests

永 A meal is served by the host

永 The scroll is replaced by flowers and, again, must be admired by the guests

永 The tea is served in the tea bowl and passed to the guests in turn

永 The rim of the bowl is wiped before being passed to the next guest

永 When drinking, guests turn the bowl slightly to avoid drinking from the front side

永 When the guests have finished their tea, the scoop, tea bowl, and whisk are rinsed by the host and all are admired

永 Before departing, guests are served a thin tea and sweets

永 About two or three days following the ceremony, guests should call or write a note of thanks to their host. This "thanking afterward" is called "korei."

WHO'S BURIED WHERE?

Corsier-sur-Vevey Cemetery,
Corsier-sur-Vevey, Switzerland
Charlie Chaplin

Forest Lawn Memorial Park,
Glendale, California
Walt Disney
Clark Gable
Spencer Tracy

Graceland Mansion Estates,
Memphis, Tennessee
Elvis Presley

Greenwood Memorial Park, Renton,
Kings Co., Washington
Jimi Hendrix

Highgate Cemetery, London, UK
George Eliot (Mary Ann Evans)
Karl Marx
Christina Rossetti

Hollywood Forever Cemetery,
California
John Houston
Tyrone Power
Rudolph Valentino

Mount Carmel Cemetery,
Hillside, Cook Co., Illinois
Al Capone

Père Lachaise, Paris, France
Sarah Bernhardt
Frederic Chopin
Edith Piaf
Jim Morrison
Marcel Proust
Oscar Wilde

Spencer Estate Grounds, Althorp,
Lake Isla, Great Brington, UK
Diana Spencer (Princess Diana)

Westminster Cathedral, Poet's
Corner, London, UK
Geoffrey Chaucer*
Robert Browning
Charles Dickens
Rudyard Kipling
Thomas Hardy
Dr. Samuel Johnson

Westwood Memorial Park,
Los Angeles, California
Marilyn Monroe

* *Chaucer was the first person to be buried in Poet's Corner, not because he was a poet but because he was clerk of works for the Palace of Westminster.*

SCHOOLS OF ARCHITECTURE

Art Deco Angles, curves, sunbursts, and pinnacles, in glass or steel.
EXAMPLE: *The Chrysler Building, New York*

Baroque Classicism with ornate decoration and complex shapes, often deliberately out of classical proportion—architecture as theater.
EXAMPLE: *St Peter's, Rome, Italy*

Classical A lot of columns, pediments, and arches, well-proportioned, made from large blocks of stone.
EXAMPLES: *The Parthenon, Athens, Greece; the Pantheon, Rome, Italy.*

Classicism/Neoclassicism Revival of classical style and order.
EXAMPLE: *The White House, Washington, DC*

Gothic Vaults, flying buttresses, pointed arches, and windows. Ornate. Big windows to let in the light.
EXAMPLE: *Chartres Cathedral, France*

Gothic Revival Faux-Gothic, often using the advances of the Industrial Revolution to create light and high spaces.
EXAMPLE: *The Houses of Parliament, London, UK*

High-Tech Deliberately futuristic, using glass and steel. Internal features, such as heating pipes and ducts, deliberately exposed.
EXAMPLE: *Lloyd's Building, London, UK*

Modernism Glass, steel, and concrete. Stark shapes. Austere.
EXAMPLE: *Guggenheim Museum, New York*

Romanesque Barrel vaults, columns, and gargoyles.
EXAMPLE: *Durham Cathedral, UK*

A RAINBOW OF NAMES

First name	Sex	Origin	Meaning
Amber	F	American	Golden
Aneurin	M	Welsh	Truly golden
Arianwen	F	Welsh	Silver
Aurelia	F	Latin	Golden
Bianca	F	Spanish	White
Blanche	F	French	White
Bronwen	F	Celtic	White-breasted
Bruno	M	German	Brown
Candida	F	Latin	White
Cerise	F	French	Cherry-red
Cherry	F	English	Cherry-red
Chloe	F	Greek	Young green shoot
Dougal	M	Celtic	Black stranger
Fenella	F	Celtic	White-shouldered
Fiona	F	Gaelic	White girl
Flavia	F	Latin	Yellow
Ginger	M/F	English	Red-haired
Gwynne	F	Celtic	White
Iris	F	Greek	Rainbow
Lloyd	M	Celtic	Grey
Melanie	F	Greek	Black
Nigel	M	Latin	Black
Phineas	M	Egyptian	Black
Rosa	F	Italian	Pink/rose
Rowena	F	Welsh	White skirt
Rory	M	Celtic	Red king
Roy	M	Celtic	Red
Rufus	M	Latin	Red-haired
Russell	M	Old French	Redhead
Scarlett	F	English	Deep red
Vanora	F	Celtic	White wave
Winifred	F	Celtic	White stream
Winne	F	Celtic	White
Xanthe	F	Greek	Yellow

SERENDIPITOUS INVENTIONS

Black rubber tires Rubber car tires were originally white—until the Goodrich tire company added black pigment so their tires wouldn't look dirty. Surprisingly, the black carbon pigment made the tires more durable. Soon all tires became black.

Chewing gum While experimenting with ways of using the traditional Mexican gum chicle as a substitute for rubber in toys, boots, and clothes, inventor Thomas Adams absentmindedly popped a piece in his mouth and was suddenly struck by the possibility of adding artificial flavor.

Potato chips In 1853 Native American chef George Crum, working in Saratoga Springs, New York, was frustrated by a guest who kept sending back his french fried potatoes, saying they were too thick. In a fit of pique, Crum cut them into wafer-thin strips and fried them. They became a house speciality.

Microwave oven Microwave generators called magnetrons were invented during World War II by scientists working on radar. Later, scientist Percy LeBaron Spencer discovered that microwaves from a magnetron had melted a chocolate bar in his pocket. The first commercial microwave oven was on the market by 1954.

Post-it notes While working on chemical formulae for stronger glues, Spencer Silver, a researcher for the 3M office-equipment company, accidentally discovered a super-weak glue. It was dismissed as useless, until a colleague, Arthur Fry, thought of applying strips of it to paper.

Safety glass Discovered by French scientist Edouard Benedictus in 1903 after he knocked a bottle of laboratory chemicals off a shelf and found the glass did not shatter—the cellulose nitrate within the bottle had coated the inside and prevented it from breaking.

HOW MANY CALORIES WILL YOU USE?

Any activity, even just lying in bed, burns calories, but some burn more than others. To burn fat, you need to do some type of aerobic exercise three times a week, for at least 20 minutes, at a rate that gets your heart beating faster (but first see your doctor for a checkup). See below to discover how many calories you may be burning.

Activity	Calories burned	Special equipment
Badminton	335	Racquet, shuttlecock
Dancing: disco, ballroom, or square	409	Partner
Bicycling: 16–19 mph	893	Bicycle
Bicycling, moderate stationary	521	Stationary bicycle
Cooking	186	None
Low-impact aerobics	409	None
Mowing lawn	335	Lawnmower
Planting shrubs	298	Garden tools
Jogging	630	Running shoes
Lying in bed	60	None
Vigorous play with kids	372	Children
Skiing, downhill	446	Skis, boots, poles
Squash	600	Racquet, ball
Standing	93	None
Swimming laps	744	Goggles, pool
Tennis	521	Racquet, ball
Walking, 4 mph	335	None

GUITARISTS' NICKNAMES FOR THEIR FAVORITE GUITARS

Guitarist	Guitar make	Nickname
Eric Clapton	Fender Strat	Blackie
Billy Gibbons (from ZZ Top)	Les Paul	Pearly Gates
B.B. King	Gibson E5355	Lucille

AMERICAN STATES AND THEIR CAPITALS

State	Capital
Alabama	Montgomery
Alaska	Juneau
Arizona	Phoenix
Arkansas	Little Rock
California	Sacramento
Colorado	Denver
Connecticut	Hartford
Delaware	Dover
Florida	Tallahassee
Georgia	Atlanta
Hawaii	Honolulu
Idaho	Boise
Illinois	Springfield
Indiana	Indianapolis
Iowa	Des Moines
Kansas	Topeka
Kentucky	Frankfort
Louisiana	Baton Rouge
Maine	Augusta
Maryland	Annapolis
Massachusetts	Boston
Michigan	Lansing
Minnesota	St Paul
Mississippi	Jackson
Missouri	Jefferson City
Montana	Helena
Nebraska	Lincoln
Nevada	Carson City
New Hampshire	Concord
New Jersey	Trenton
New Mexico	Santa Fe
New York	Albany
North Carolina	Raleigh
North Dakota	Bismarck
Ohio	Columbus
Oklahoma	Oklahoma City
Oregon	Salem
Pennsylvania	Harrisburg
Rhode Island	Providence
South Carolina	Columbia
South Dakota	Pierre
Tennessee	Nashville
Texas	Austin
Utah	Salt Lake City
Vermont	Montpelier
Virginia	Richmond
Washington	Olympia
West Virginia	Charleston
Wisconsin	Madison
Wyoming	Cheyenne

THE FLAG OF THE UNITED STATES OF AMERICA

Known as "The Stars and Stripes," the US flag has 13 alternating horizontal stripes (7 red, 6 white). A panel of blue with 50 white stars (one per state) appears in the top corner on the hoist side.

STAR WARS WHO'S WHO

EPISODE IV—*A New Hope* (1977)

Heroes Luke (Mark Hamill), Leia (Carrie Fisher), Han Solo (Harrison Ford), Chewbacca (Peter Mayhew), Obi-Wan Kenobi (Alec Guinness), C-3PO (Anthony Daniels), R2-D2 (Kenny Baker), the droids

Villains Darth Vader (Dave Prowse, voiced by James Earl Jones), Grand Moff Tarkin (Peter Cushing)

EPISODE V— *The Empire Strikes Back* (1980)

Heroes Luke, Leia, Han, Chewbacca, the droids, Yoda (voiced by Frank Oz), Lando (Billy Dee Williams)

Villains Darth Vader, Boba Fett (Jeremy Bulloch), Lando

EPISODE VI—*Return of the Jedi* (1983)

Heroes Luke, Leia, Han, Chewbacca, the droids, Lando, the Ewoks, the Mon Calamari.

Villains Boba Fett, Jabba the Hutt, Darth Vader (played by Sebastian Shaw when unmasked as Anakin Skywalker), the Emperor (Ian McDiarmid)

EPISODE I— *The Phantom Menace* (1999)

Heroes Qui Gon Jinn (Liam Neeson), Obi-Wan Kenobi (Ewan McGregor), Anakin Skywalker (Jake Lloyd), Queen Amidala (Natalie Portman), R2-D2, C-3PO, Jar-Jar Binks (Ahmed Best)

Villains Darth Sidious (Uncredited), Darth Maul (Ray Park), the Trade Federation

EPISODE II—*Attack of the Clones* (2002)

Heroes Obi-Wan Kenobi, Anakin Skywalker (Hayden Christensen), Padme Amidala, R2-D2, C-3PO, Yoda, Mace Windu (Samuel L. Jackson)

Villains Darth Sidious, Count Dooku/Darth Tyrannus (Christopher Lee), Jango Fett (Temuera Morrison)

EPISODE III—*(as yet untitled)*: release date: 2005.

PEOPLE WHO GAVE THEIR NAMES TO THINGS

Invention	*Inventor*	*Date*
BRAILLE	Louis Braille (1809–52)	1829

Story: He invented the system of raised type for blind people.

| CARDIGAN | James Thomas Brudenell (1797–1868) 7th Earl of Cardigan | 1850s |

Story: His long-sleeved wool vest was eponymously named after the leader of the "Charge of the Light Brigade," at Balaclava in 1854.

| DECIBEL | Alexander Graham Bell (1847–1922) | 1900s |

Story: Unit of acoustic power named after inventor of the telephone, based on Bell's research into sound, resonance, and communication.

| DIESEL ENGINE | Rudolph Diesel (1858–1913) | 1895 |

Story: His "rational heat motor" was the first compression-ignition engine to be used.

| LISTERINE | Dr. Joseph Lister (1827–1912) | 1879 |

Story: Lister was the first to use an antiseptic during surgery. Later, the Missouri physician Dr. Joseph Lawrence refined the product to form the now famous mouthwash, which he named after Lister.

| MACINTOSH | Charles Macintosh (1766–1843) | 1823 |

Story: While researching byproducts of the coal-gas process, he came across dissolved india rubber and made the first waterproof cloth.

| PASTEURIZATION | Louis Pasteur (1822–95) | 1860s |

Story: His "germ theory" gave rise to pasteurization, vaccination, anti-septic operations, and paved the way for modern biology and biochemistry.

| SANDWICH | John Montagu (1718–92) 4th Earl of Sandwich | 1762 |

Story: His "sandwich" (a piece of salt beef between two slices of toasted bread) let him remain at the gambling table while eating.

STRANGE DEATHS OF SOME POPES

Stephen VII (896–897)   Attacked, jailed, and strangled

John X (914–928)   Imprisoned and suffocated

John XIII (956–972)   Bludgeoned to death on the way to see
                             his lady-in-waiting by her husband

John XIV (983–984)   Left to die of starvation in prison

John XXI (1276–1277)   Died when the roof of his new study
                             fell on him

LIFE CYCLE OF A FROG

Frogs hibernate underground, emerging in spring to mate. The male fertilizes the female's eggs as they are laid, and after a couple of weeks, the tadpoles, fishlike animals with long tails, external gills, and no limbs, hatch. Over the next three to four months, the external gills are replaced by internal gills and lungs, the hind legs and the front legs develop, then finally, the tail shrinks and disappears. The adult frog is now ready to emerge onto land.

THE GREAT LAKES

Lake	Area
Superior	32,140 sq miles/83,270 sq km
Huron	23,430 sq miles/60,700 sq km
Michigan	22,395 sq miles/58,020 sq km
Erie	9,915 sq miles/25,680 sq km
Ontario	7,425 sq miles/19,230 sq km

JAZZ LINGO

Expression	Meaning	Expression	Meaning
Air check	Recording of a TV or radio performance	Doghouse	String bass
		Gig	A paid music job
Bad	Good	Gitter	Guitar
Barn Burner	Something (originally a woman) of high quality	Gobble pipe	Saxophone
		Groanbox	Accordion
		Hide hitter	Drummer
		Iron horn	Cornet
Blow	Play an instrument	Supermurgitroid	Ultra cool
Boogie man	Jazz critic	Tin ear	A nonmusic fan
Cat	One who plays jazz	Tram	Trombone
Clinker	A bad note	Wax a disc	Cut a record
Daddy-o	Hipster term of address	Wig out	To get upset
		Woodshed	To practice

NEW YORK AVENUES FROM EAST TO WEST

HUDSON RIVER (West Side Highway) — 12th Avenue ← → 11th Avenue — 10th Avenue — 9th Avenue — 8th Avenue — 7th Avenue — Broadway* — 6th Avenue (Avenue of the Americas) — 5th Avenue — Madison Avenue — Park Avenue — Lexington Avenue — 3rd Avenue — 2nd Avenue — 1st Avenue ← → FDR Drive → EAST RIVER

Originally an Indian trail, Broadway is the only avenue that runs diagonally. It is on the West Side above 23rd Street and east of 5th Avenue below.

FAMOUS NICKNAMES

If the old maxim is true that you only know you have become truly famous when you have acquired a nickname, the recipients of some of the less flattering sobriquets below probably wish they had remained in obscurity.

Nickname	Real name
Bard of Twickenham, The	Alexander Pope
Big Ben	Sir Benjamin Hall*
Billy the Kid	William H. Bonney
Bohemian Corporal, The	Adolf Hitler
Boss, The	Bruce Springsteen
Dizzy	Benjamin Disraeli
Flanders Mare, The	Anne of Cleves
Great Beast, The	Aleister Crowley
Groover from Vancouver, The	Bryan Adams
Hammer of the Scots, The	Edward I (warmongering monarch)
Honest Abe	President Abraham Lincoln
Iron Duke, The	Arthur Wellesley, Duke of Wellington
Iron Lady, The	Margaret Thatcher
Lionheart	Richard I
Lucky Lindy	Charles Lindbergh
Muscles from Brussels, The	Jean-Claude Van Damme
Old Hickory	US President Andrew Jackson
Slowhand	Eric Clapton
Supermac	Harold Macmillan
Tricky Dicky	US President Richard Nixon
Virgin Queen, The	Elizabeth I

* A rotund commissioner of clocks

THE FLAG OF LIBYA

The Libyan flag is a plain dark green only, with green being the traditional color of Islam.

STONEHENGE

Located on Salisbury Plain in southern England, the megalithic monument of Stonehenge is an impressive configuration of huge stone slabs arranged in a circular formation. Stonehenge was probably built toward the end of the second millennium BC and consists of several trilithons (two stones topped by a third). The stones are arranged in a series: the two outer groups form circles; the third and fourth groups form a horseshoe shape. Within the curve of the horseshoe is the altar stone. Most archaeologists agree that Stonehenge was used for religious purposes. However, it is also possible that it was used as a huge astronomical instrument since the midsummer sunrise is aligned with its axis.

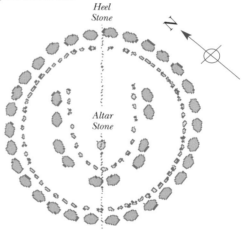

Heel Stone

Altar Stone

N

THE FLAG OF HONDURAS

The flag of Honduras is divided into three horizontal bands. The top and bottom bands are blue, while the middle band is white and bears five blue stars in the center.

THE STRANGE DEATHS OF ROMAN EMPERORS

Caligula (r.37–41)

After leaving the Palatine Games, Caligula was attacked in a narrow passageway by members of a senate/praetorian conspiracy. His throat was slashed and his chest stabbed and there were 30 other wounds. His wife and daughter were also killed later that day.

Claudius (r.41–54)

He was already very ill, but impatient wife Agrippina had the poisoner Locusta (officially employed by the palace!) poison a mushroom. Lest this should fail, Agrippina had the doctor (Xenophon) put more of the poison down the emperor's throat—on the feather being used to cause him to vomit up the first poison!

Tiberius (r.14–37)

According to a story by Tacitus (*c.* 55–120), Tiberius appeared to die and his successor Caligula removed the ring from his finger only to have Tiberius reveal himself as not quite dead. Macro, the praetorian commander, then smothered him with a cushion.

Vitellius (r.69)

After defeat by an army of Vespasians, Vitellius disguised himself as a beggar. However, the Flavians (Vespasian's men) found, tortured, and killed him and dumped him in the Tiber.

FAMOUS SINGING DRUMMERS

Name	*Band*
Karen Carpenter	The Carpenters
Phil Collins	Genesis, then went solo
Stewart Copeland	The Police
Mickey Dolenz	The Monkees
Kevin Godley	10cc, Roxy Music, Godley & Creme
Don Henley	The Eagles, then went solo
Keith Moon	The Who
Ringo Starr	The Beatles

VITAMINS

Vitamin	RDI	Sources	All in one go!*
A	5,000 IU	Meat, liver, dairy, dark green, orange, and yellow vegetables	2½ oz (60 g) carrots
Thiamin	1.5 mg	Cereals, nuts, legumes, pork	6½ oz (130 g) peanuts
Riboflavin	1.7 mg	Dairy, meat, fish, asparagus, spinach, yeast extract	⅝ oz (13 g) yeast extract
Niacin	20 mg	Meat and cereals	4 oz (80 g) chicken
B_6	2 mg	Poultry, fish, pork, oats, peanuts	2½ oz (60 g) wheatgerm
Folic Acid	0.4 mg	Leafy vegetables, yeast extract, liver	20 spears asparagus
B_{12}	6 mcg	Any animal-derived food, including dairy	18 oz (360 g) cooked haddock
C	60 mg	Fruits and vegetables	2½ oz (50 g) green peppers
D	400 IU	Fatty fish, eggs, margarine (also made by the body with sufficient exposure to UV rays in sunlight)	2½ oz (50 g) grilled salmon
E	80 IU	Vegetable oil, nuts, vegetables, cereals	2 oz (40 g) shelled hazelnuts
K	not known	Leafy dark green vegetables	n/a

* Although you can get all your RDIs (recommended daily intakes, which has replaced the US RDAs) from a single food, it's best to eat a balanced diet.

** IU = International Units; mcg = microgram

MINERALS

Mineral	RDA	Sources	All in one go!*
Calcium	1 g	Dairy products, seaweed, some vegetables	5 oz (135 g) full fat Cheddar cheese
Iron	18 mg	Red meat, dark green vegetables, herbs	1 lb 9 oz (845 g) of lean beef
Magnesium	400 mg	Nuts and seeds, green vegetables	5 oz (145 g) cashew nuts
Potassium	n/a	Fruit, legumes, nuts, onions, potatoes, bananas, other fruits and vegetables	n/a
Selenium	n/a	Brazil nuts, fish	n/a
Sodium	n/a	Most processed foods, vegetables	n/a
Zinc	15 mg	Meat and dairy, cereals	2 oysters

GOLF BALLS THROUGH THE YEARS

Feathery Leather covered, stuffed with "a gentleman's top hat full" of feathers.

Gutta-percha First made in 1848 by Dr. Robert Adams Peterson from gutta-percha (the evaporated milky juice from a Malaysian tree).

Hand-hammered gutta A gutta-percha hand-hammered with a sharp-edged hammer to make it fly better.

Bramble Textures and patterns were pressed into gutta-perchas to make them fly as well as the hand-hammered balls, but at less cost.

Rubber ball Rubber thread around a solid rubber core. Invented in 1898 by Coburn Haskell of Cleveland, Ohio, USA.

Solid core (two-piece) A large solid rubber ball covered by a dimpled plastic coating.

Three-piece A small solid or liquid-filled core wrapped around with tens of yards of rubber cord and then wrapped in dimpled plastic.

SIGN LANGUAGE ALPHABET

Sign language is a form of visual communication that has its own grammar, structure, and word order which is different from English. There are as many sign languages as there are spoken languages, i.e. French Sign Language, American Sign Language (usually abbreviated to ASL), Australian Sign Language (also known as Auslan), Spanish Sign Language, Japanese Sign Language, etc.

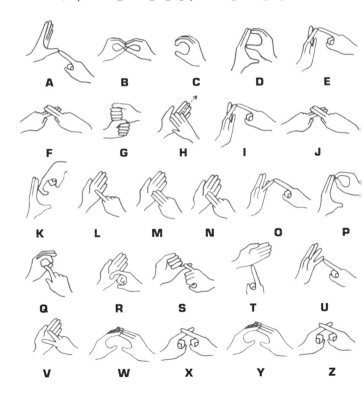

ABBREVIATIONS OF AMERICAN STATES

State	Abbreviation	State	Abbreviation
Alabama	AL	Montana	MT
Alaska	AK	Nebraska	NE
Arizona	AZ	Nevada	NV
Arkansas	AR	New Hamspire	NH
California	CA	New Jersey	NJ
Colorado	CO	New Mexico	NM
Connecticut	CT	New York	NY
Delaware	DE	North Carolina	NC
Florida	FL	North Dakota	ND
Georgia	GA	Ohio	OH
Hawaii	HI	Oklahoma	OK
Idaho	ID	Oregon	OR
Illinois	IL	Pennsylvania	PA
Indiana	IN	Rhode Island	RI
Iowa	IA	South Carolina	SC
Kansas	KS	South Dakota	SD
Kentucky	KY	Tennessee	TN
Louisiana	LA	Texas	TX
Maine	ME	Utah	UT
Maryland	MD	Vermont	VT
Massachusetts	MA	Virginia	VA
Michigan	MI	Wasington	WA
Minnesota	MN	West Virginia	WV
Mississippi	MS	Wisconsin	WI
Missouri	MO	Wyoming	WY

Washington, the national capital of the United States of America, is not located in a state, but in a neutral district—the District of Columbia, which is abbreviated "DC."

ALL THE TIME THERE IS

The prehistory of the Earth is divided into Eons, Eras, Periods, and Epochs. Almost the entire history of multicellular life has occurred within the Phanerozoic Eon, comprising the past 540 million years.

The Eons

Hadean Eon (4,600 million years ago [mya] to 3,800 mya)

Archaean Eon (3,800 mya to 2,500 mya)

Proterozoic Eon (2,500 mya to 540 mya), includes three Eras:
• Palaeoproterozoic Era (2,500 mya to 1,600 mya)
• Mesoproterozoic Era (1,600 mya to 900 mya)
• Neoproterozoic Era (900 mya to 540 mya), includes one Period:
• Vendian Period (650 mya to 540 mya: *first signs of multicellular life*)

Phanerozoic Eon (540 mya to present: *see opposite*)

TIMESCALE OF LIFE

If the 4.6 billion years since the Earth's formation were crammed into the thousand years from AD 1000 to the eve of 2000, it would yield the following dates:

1000 Formation of the Earth
1173 First life appears
1543 First single-celled organisms with a nucleus appear
1843 Multicellular animals appear
1891 The first land plants appear
1950S TO MID-1980S The age of the dinosaurs
MID-DECEMBER 1999 Early modern man, *Homo sapiens*, appear
AROUND DECEMBER 22, 1999 The emergence of modern man:
                    Homo sapiens sapiens.

PHANEROZOIC EON (540 MYA TO PRESENT)

Palaeozoic Era (540 mya to 250 mya)

Cambrian Period (540 mya to 500 mya):	*First vertebrates appear*
Ordovician Period (500 mya to 435 mya):	*First jawed fishes*
Silurian Period (435 mya to 410 mya):	*First plants and arthropods colonize land*
Devonian Period (410 mya to 355 mya):	*Age of fishes, first four-limbed vertebrates*
Carboniferous Period (355 mya to 295 mya):	*Swamps, early amphibians, and giant insects*
Permian Period (295 to 250 mya):	*Mammallike reptiles dominate*

Mesozoic Era (250 to 65 mya)

Triassic Period (250 mya to 203 mya):	*First dinosaurs and other "archosaurs" appear*
Jurassic Period (203 mya to 135 mya):	*Early heyday of dinosaurs—first birds evolve*
Cretaceous Period (135 mya to 65 mya):	*Last of dinosaurs—duck bills, tyrannosaurs, horned dinosaurs*

Cenozoic Era (65 mya to present)

Tertiary Period (65 mya to 1.75 mya)

Palaeocene Epoch (65 mya to 53 mya):	*Mammals diversify and grow*
Eocene Epoch (53 mya to 33.7 mya):	*First horses, elephants, and whales*
Oligocene Epoch (33.7 mya to 23.5 mya):	*First monkeys, deer*
Miocene Epoch (23.5 mya to 5.4 mya):	*First apes*
Pliocene Epoch (5.4 mya to 1.75 mya):	*Grazing mammals, such as cattle and sheep, evolve*
Pleistocene Epoch: (1.75 mya to 10,000 years ago)	*Ice-age giant mammals, modern humans evolve*

Quaternary Period (1.75 mya to present)

Holocene Epoch: (10,000 years ago to present)	*Humans dominate the planet and begin to cause extinctions*

INDEX